Deep Calls Unto Deep

Reflections on the intersecting lives and writings of Fred Buechner, Tony Abbott, and Louis Patrick

D0862120

With gratitude! Love, Janet
July 14, 2021

Janet Vass Sarjeant

Parson's Porch Books

Deep Calls Unto Deep
ISBN: Softcover 978-1-955581-03-5
Copyright © 2021 by Janet Vass Sarjeant

Parson's Porch Books is an imprint of Parson's Porch & Company (PP&C) in Cleveland, Tennessee. PP&C is an innovative organization which raises money by publishing books of noted authors, representing all genres. Its face and voice is **David Russell Tullock** (dtullock@parsonsporch.com).

Parson's Porch & Company *turns books into bread & milk* by sharing its profits with the poor.

www.parsonsporch.com

Deep Calls Unto Deep

Deep calls unto deep at the thunder of thy cataracts. Psalm 42:7

Prologue

No one escapes. From the beginning, men and women "are born to trouble as sparks fly upward." These words from Job speak to us from the form of an ancient poem, a universal cry against the troubles and the fires and the travails of being human. That poet wrote out of that anguish. The writer Red Smith is quoted saying, "Writing is easy, all you have to do is sit down at the typewriter, cut open a vein, and bleed." To what end, we may ask? The sound of their own cry to the heavens? For surely the words are sent heavenward, just as sparks rise from the fires here on this earth into the air above. Do the words cry out for justice and help from God? Do they cry out because we need to share our miseries with other humans? All of the above, I imagine.

There is something else, however, that comes from these writings and travails. *We* the listeners are lifted up like the sparks, but in life-affirming ways. We who hear the words are willing to journey with the writer, maybe into the darkest of darkness, and then, mysteriously, we are loosened from some of the burdens of our own journeys. They are wonderful, these written words, because these writers imagine that God the Divine is calling from just such depths as these, that deep calls unto deep. The writer of Job imagined it so. He cries (or maybe he whispers) that God's calling to us, these words which include the recounting of God's mighty acts, "are too wonderful for me."

The lives and the writings of three men who write out of just such depths, just such longings, are intertwined. H. Louis Patrick, Frederick Buechner, and Tony Abbott became friends; these three men became influencers; these three men wrote of a journey towards God, no matter the depth of their darkness.

Lou Patrick

"Of the uncounted places I have lived in, for years or months, only one haunts me. Since I left it for good, I have been adrift, and shall drift to my death. Yet I cannot go back there—any more than a tree, cut down, could return to its roots left in the ground."—from *Journey from the North* by Storm Jameson

Lou Patrick says this to me in a recorded dialogue from 1996: "Home is a place—outwardly. But inside it is a time that is before time." That home for Lou Patrick is Newberry, SC, where he was born on August 2, 1921. Only son of Azile Parr and Andrew Patrick, his first 11 years were spent in Newberry, surrounded by a community of many family members and many friends. It was a time of attending the Associate Reformed Presbyterian Church with many of his family. But in 1933, when his parents divorced, Lou's mother took him to Washington, DC, to live, and he knew *no one* there but his mother—this after a lifetime of knowing and belonging to the Newberry community. From that interview of 1996, Lou says, "I remember as an 11-year-old leaving home. Nobody knew it, but I went back to the place to visit, and I cried my eyes out, because there would never be another place, couldn't be another place and be 'home.'" This is the 'outward' home. The place of your childhood which you can't have again because you are not a child. A place, as Lou says, for which you will always be homesick. But the home you carry with you, he believed, is the home you spend your life trying to grow up to with what you stored up as a child. As Lou grew, his new days

9

in Washington, DC, were filled with school, movies (lots of movies), and life with his single mother. And, interestingly, when it was time for college, Lou returned to South Carolina to attend Erskine College in Due West, SC, where others in his family had matriculated. His college was founded in the Associate Reformed Presbyterian tradition of Evangelical Calvinist doctrine. He received his Bachelor of Arts in 1942. Did he know then that he wanted to be a minister? Probably. We talked once of how much easier it was to not have to decide what your vocation would be. I always knew I would be a teacher; he always knew he would be a preacher. He told me that even as a child in Newberry, he was called 'Preacher,' but I can't remember if he told me what he did to earn this nickname. I picture this redheaded child/preacher standing on familiar streets professing something!! What would he profess, I wonder? Who knows? But we do know that after Erskine College, he decided to attend Princeton Theological Seminary where he earned a Master of Theology degree. This is the destiny Lou Patrick chose. This is the gladness even in the face of darkness and death, that Lou Patrick chose. The choice that one must give one's all when Jesus says, "Come." And like Peter, who responds to Jesus and in faith leaps into the Sea of Galilee, Lou gathered up his yesterdays and all his tomorrows and risked them for the sake of this summons.

When America entered World War II, Lou Patrick served as a Marine Corps Chaplain. One of Lou's favorite references to life aboard the ship in the Pacific Theater became an allusion used in several instances in sermons. One such sermon I

10

remember dealt with the power of "hearing" as it pertains to the Word of God. Lou would chuckle as he remembered that voice over the ship's intercom calmly yet unrelentingly saying, "Now hear this. Now hear this." He said that when Marines heard the announcement, they had better *listen* and then they better *do* what was commanded. Lou likened it to the old Hebrew for 'word': *davar.* The Hebrew definition is 'a command.' Lou believed that if one heard, really heard the commands of the captain, and, analogously, if one really heard the commands of God, then one should act. He thought it served well in the Marine Corps. He thought it served God.

After returning home from the war, Lou Patrick married Elizabeth Plaxco in 1946. Together they embarked on a life with academic beginnings from Erskine College where they met, to Princeton University, and onward. Lou took graduate courses at Colombia University and Union Theological Seminary in New York before taking his first calling to be pastor at First Statesville Church, an ARP Church in Statesville, NC. Doris Betts, one of his parishioners there, became a best-selling author, and she dedicated one of her books to Lou Patrick, calling him "The whale-tale preacher of my youth." They kept in touch through the years. What did Ms. Betts hear from that pulpit in Statesville that rang in her ears always? The phrase she used about Lou somewhat answers that question. The size of the stories in the Bible, the size of the stories he used in his preaching, the size of the man himself were all big (Lou Patrick had the large physique of many in his family line of SC Parr men—large and rotund). Lou's sermons were "whale-sized." As an illustration of the preacher, he was even in the beginning, I think the Methodist preacher, author, and academician William H. Willimon hits the mark. He refers to this bigger-than-life quality of Lou Patrick in an article written in 1987 called "Poetic Preachers." Willimon says a definition of heaven is a "place where everyone talks like H. Louis Patrick." He goes on to say Lou "uses a muscular English that is poetic . . . every word is correctly placed. His sermons are Matthew, Mark, and Luke filtered through Frost, Sandburg, and C.S. Lewis. He sounds like God, if God were fortunate enough to have a good bass voice and to have been from Due West, South Carolina." As a preacher of the Word, the price of writing and giving of this Word is a heavy one sometimes. But perhaps the rewards are there, too. As Willimon writes, "As long as there is one person left to tell the Story, and tell it well, to consider heaven and hell hung between a mere word and the exact word, then all of us have hope." Willimon, a writer about the Word himself, just might know something of this!

So, what of this heavy price? What of the darkness that is inherent in telling the Story of God and Man-and-Womankind even though the story is ultimately good news? Lou Patrick's favorite Psalm was #42. He used it over and over again in sermons and in talks with parishioners who sat across the desk from him in his study.

"As a hart longs
for flowing streams,
so longs my soul
for thee, O God. . .
Why are you Cast down, O my soul,
and why are you disquieted within me?
Hope in God; for I shall again praise him,
my help and my God."

The poet is cast down, but hope is rock-solid in God. Why?
Because when we travel to the deepest part of ourselves,
perhaps even rock bottom, there is where God and humankind
meet.

"Deep calls unto deep
at the thunder of thy cataracts;
all thy waves and thy billows
have gone over me.
By day the Lord commands his steadfast love;
and at night his song is with me,
a prayer to the God of my life."

Lou Patrick believed in this "deepening." And this 'deep'
usually meant an accompanying darkness.

In a sermon of his from 1976, Lou starts with these words:
"Ever since I was a child, I have been strangely haunted by
these words out of Psalm 42—the 7th verse: 'Deep calls unto
deep at the thunder of Thy cataracts, Oh God.'" Lou goes on

in the sermon to say that he knows that the psalmist who wrote this poem "was in exile in the rugged peaks of Mount Hermon and Mount Mizar, the peaks where the River Jordan has its rise. The poet is listening to the River surging through those mountain passages with its awful thunder. He is missing his village; he is missing home." This sermon uses the idea and the reality Lou has been fashioning his whole life of the price humans pay when leaving the 'time before time' which is the childhood home and heading into the world that is measured in time—birth to death. Lou says, "You leave the village (home) and go up into the gaps where the mysteries are, where the real questions are." He ends this sermon by saying "Now this is why we come to worship. We come because the deep in us hears the call of the deep in the unsearchable judgements of God whose ways are not the village ways . . . we do not come into the presence of this God by the step-by-step logic of discovering his ways . . . There is no way to Him except to stand in the gaps and hear the thunder of His cataracts, and nowhere is the sound so clear as in the coming of the one called Jesus. . . [God] can bring to us this ultimate mystery of One who so lived and died here that in him sound the very deeps of God. Nowhere does Jesus supply explanations to the question of pain and sin and death. He simply bore them and lived them and triumphed over them. There is no other way to live in the mystery where the deep calls unto the deep except to stand lost in wonder and love and praise before the thunder of God's cataracts, not the sound of ours." THIS is the encapsulated message of Lou Patrick as a preacher and writer. He preaches this personal word of belief: "That's why the Bible

14

is always echoing this thunder. Always!" Lou reworked this sermon in 1991 and writes that he had had to memorize Psalm 42 as a child. "I didn't understand the words then. I don't understand them now. All I know is they voice my feelings when the joys and sorrows of life overwhelm me."

Perhaps his first taste of how dark this world can be started with the divorce of his parents. But he was surely plunged into the deepest of his darknesses by the drowning death of his six-year-old son Henry in 1956. Lou and Elizabeth Patrick, along with children Jane, Mary, and Henry, had gathered with extended family at Lake Murray in South Carolina. Henry, while playing with his sisters and cousins by the lake, slipped into a deeper part of the lake, unnoticed at first. He was found an hour later but was unable to be resuscitated. The darkness surrounding an event like this, in anyone's life, seems impenetrable. The coping mechanisms for humans in such times must vary almost person to person. Lou coped by rarely speaking of it, not to his wife, not to his daughters, not to his parishioners. His daughter Jane Patrick Findlay told me that the children rarely brought up the name of their brother Henry to their parents because of the pain it caused. Elizabeth said the same thing to me, but said she liked saying Henry's name aloud to me and other close friends; it brought him near again, she said. Elizabeth also told me that she feared that in heaven, Henry would be so near to the 'light' of God that she couldn't get to him. What a fear to have.

In the Trinity Presbyterian manse in Charlotte, NC, where the Patricks lived for about 40 years, a huge painting of Henry covered a wall on the upstairs landing, so of course that was a daily reminder of their red-headed son and brother. And of course, they wanted to remember, but Lou buried the pain so deep within himself that it was hardly allowed to be worded. But darkness, the discussion of the deepest darkness of all and how God is there calling out from the deep, that darkness with God in it, is mentioned over and over again in Lou's writings. Oh, there are some who wanted him to 'lighten up," to preach a happier message. Lou tells the story of one such parishioner in a 1978 sermon entitled "After Bethlehem, What?" The person said, "you're not putting light at the end of the tunnel. You are not promising us that for which we are looking and for which we are waiting. You are draping the doors of the church with crepe and mourning. Give us some joy and peace and hope. . . That's why PTL (*Praise the Lord*—an evangelical ministry near Charlotte, NC) makes it, and why shouldn't we make it likewise?" Another young parishioner told me once that she was tired of "gloom and doom, Lou." But for those types of people, those quoting the praise psalms of joy, joy, joy, there are many more who in Walter Brueggemann's words identify with the Psalms that are "experiences of being overwhelmed, nearly destroyed, and surprisingly given life which empower us to pray and sing,"(1) Psalms that take us down into the pit of darkness before coming up to the light. In that same 1978 sermon, Lou says: "Always we go from Bethlehem to bedlam." He goes on to say that the day after

Christmas is the Day of St. Stephen, who was martyred for Jesus's sake.

"As the angry mob was setting on him, he saw the heavens open and the Son of Man sitting at the right hand of God. We cannot live now under a sky without a rent in it. You can't ever see stars without being reminded of His star. You can't ever see children without being reminded of this child. . . that one event gives all that went before and after its meaning. You have to take it all together. It is a rent sky now because Bethlehem is as real as bedlam."

The next paragraph in that sermon tells of a Christmas Card that arrived from Fred Buechner. Lou describes the card as showing a room like other rooms, perhaps the living room in a farmhouse in winter. Snow is falling *inside* the house, and there are stars scattered on the floor. And yet, Lou says, "it has an unspeakable warmth, an unutterable kind of welcome." And at the bottom of the picture were Fred Buechner's handwritten words, "Love makes one little room an everywhere." Lou believes that that rent in the sky "makes all sights bearable, meaningful, significant." Even in the real world, in bedlam.

How many listeners were lifted out of the darkness and into the light of hope by Lou Patrick's words? Hundreds. Nay, thousands. Lou Patrick preached more sermons on the radio broadcast called "The Protestant Hour" than any other preacher in the history of the broadcast. Ever. To read the sermon "A Balm in Gilead," preached for The Protestant Hour on Sunday, July 8, 1956, just one month before the death of Lou Patrick's son Henry, is to feel the pulse, the very lifeblood of preaching of a balm which would have to be proven in Lou's own life, a darkness that would have to be lived, and lived through.

Lou's sermon starts with Job and the quote used to start *this* book, that "Job speaks for us all when he says, 'man is as prone to trouble as sparks are to fly upward.' Therefore, let us be kind, for everyone we meet is carrying a heavier burden than we think. When these difficulties come, they bring some dark night that engulfs our souls; doubts which rap and knock and enter our minds. . . Every black heap of sorrow brings wild entreaties to the sky. We are like infants crying in the night, crying for the light, with no language but a cry."

In this sermon, Lou seems to address the theme he will need and use and believe for the rest of his life. That the deep longing of men and women for God, and the deepness of God's love calling to men and women at that deepest level, is irrefutable. And the right words are needed to witness to this deep calling unto deep. The words are the words of poetry, that form of expression that captures the highs and the lows, the shouts and the whispers of what is meant to put God and Human in the same sentence. In this sermon of July 8, 1956, Lou quotes Edgar Allen Poe, Abraham Lincoln, Henrik Ibsen, Rabbi Hillel of the Spanish Inquisition, Thornton Wilder, Theresa of Avila, and Job, Isaiah, Daniel, and Paul from the stories of the Bible. It is as if Lou pulls out all the stops, preparing but unprepared for the event just one month hence. How to bear the unbearable darkness.

Excerpts from the sermon:

"Edgar Allan Poe experienced a haunting sorrow in the death of his beloved Lenore. The burden of that grief he poured out in his poem, "The Raven," where the bird stands for the sorrow in his heart that will leave him nevermore. The poem reaches its climax when the poet turns to the raven and exclaims,

"Prophet, thing of evil, prophet still, if bird or devil —
Whether Tempter sent, or whether tempest tossed these here ashore.
Desolate yet all undaunted, on this desert land enchanted,
In this home by horror haunted; tell me truly, I implore;
Is there—is there balm in Gilead? —Tell me —tell me, I implore."

And for Lou , who could still quote this entire poem of Poe at age 80, the answer to that cry comes not from the poem "The Raven," but "out of one of our most moving spirituals":

"'There is a balm in Gilead
that makes the wounded whole,
There is a balm in Gilead
that heals the sin-sick soul.'

He says, "This is what we need; not some explanation of some sufferings, but something to give us the grace to see them through, to strengthen us for an honorable through-bearing of them."

How that word 'through-bearing' is the exact word for us. He goes on . . .

He quotes Lincoln: "Deep scars of sorrow sat entrenched on Abraham Lincoln's face, but he could still say, "Wisdom is minted from mortal wounds." And Ibsen's character who said in response to the question 'Who taught you to sing?' said, "God sent me sorrow. Ever as the day wore on the trouble grew, wherefrom he guessed that a great good was about to be born." Lou says the deepest tragedy has no explanation. The tragedy that tears our lives to tatters, leaves us broken and bleeding, there can be no explaining of it. In this 1956 sermon, he thinks Dickens's story of Sidney Carlton in *A Tale of Two Cities* is one of the most moving in literature. When Carlton and a young girl are slated to go to their deaths by guillotine the next day, she asks, "I wonder if you would mind on the morrow, as they take us to the guillotine, if I put my hand in yours? I think it would give me courage.' And sure enough, on the morrow, as they go down the cobblestone streets in the cart together, her hand is in his. There isn't a trace of fear in her eyes as they step out of the cart and begin to climb the steps. She turns to him and says, 'You know, I think you were sent to me by God.'"

Did Lou Patrick remember this sermon of his the next month when the clouds of darkness surrounded him and his family? Did he remember from that sermon of the previous month Thornton Wilder's character who has an angel come and whisper, "Without your wound, where would your power be? It is your very regret that makes your low voice go trembling into the hearts of men. I tell you, angels in Heaven can not persuade human beings as well as someone that has been broken on the wheels of living." And in that sermon, he saves some bittersweet humor for the sermon's end, the words from Theresa of Avila: 'Oh God, why doest Thou pursue us with such pains, those of us that love Thee so?' And God answered, 'I save pains for my friends.' 'No wonder, then, Thou hast so few, she replied.' Finally, he quotes the spiritual "Balm in Gilead" again and says, "And this is it; the power of God that is present with us in our suffering, and the peace that comes to us through sharing His death and victory. Amen."

Lou Patrick's voice came trembling into so many hearts through his own brokenness and the more than five decades of choosing words. Listen to his sermon titles: "Thundering Cataracts," "The Well of Loneliness and the Waiting Heart," "The God Who Gets Hurt," "Clouds, Darkness, and the Morning Star," "The Midnight Knock." On and on go the titles of deep calling unto deep, a light in the darkness that shines in that darkness and somehow makes us feel less alone. How Lou kept his faith after the loss of his father's presence in his life and the loss of his young son can't be easily answered but there is the evidence that he kept choosing as Will

Willimon said not mere words but exact words, stringing them together in such a way as to make believers in the God of the deep of those who heard him. Hundreds of sermons profess the God of the deep calling unto the deep of our lives. Hundreds of hours of counseling men and women who sought him attest to healing powers. Lou pointed to the balm of God, his presence with us in the dark.

To go back to Lou's timeline, and after the Statesville, NC, church, the next calling came; he went to the AR Presbyterian Church of Charlotte, but he did not stay long. There was a breach of trust between that Charlotte church and Lou Patrick. He was asked to leave and henceforth chose pastorates of the Presbyterian Church and not the ARP denomination. By personality and calling, Lou Patrick spoke his mind and what he believed scriptures reveal about God, showing a liberality of thought that perhaps did not jive with the growing conservatism of the ARP. He loved music of all kinds, secular and religious, and yet only melodies set to the Psalms were allowed in the ARP church. Or was the divide triggered by the ARP standing behind the inerrancy of the Bible and ideas of conflict like the virgin birth of Jesus? For whatever reason, Lou Patrick took the pastorate of two churches in the Midwest: Westminster Presbyterian Church in St. Louis (1951-1956), MO, and Second Presbyterian Church in Kansas City, MO (1956-1962). After these pastorates, after a doctorate from Westminster College, after the death of Henry and the birth of a daughter Barbara, Lou came to Trinity Presbyterian Church in Charlotte, NC, where he stayed for three decades. Over these three decades he preached a lively word from the pulpit and taught and counseled in his spacious study. A constant aroma of pipe tobacco filled that book-lined room, and when the pipe was not being filled, he chewed the remains of a cigar. The presence of coffee was everywhere, in unwashed cups on his bookcase behind him, and in the rings those cups made on papers on his desk. If one peruses his sermon files, one sees the remnants of coffee rings on many a page. Like the coffee he stirred in his study, he so stirred up the congregants at Trinity from the beginning that tension sometimes followed. In a video for Trinity's 50th Anniversary celebration in 2001, Lou recorded some remarks for the occasion. He told the story of some elders coming to his study soon after he had arrived in 1963, bringing him the message that he was going to have to leave. Lou says one of them had a Bible in one hand while the other hand was rolled into a fist. Lou's answer, as he remembers it, was 'I just got here, and I like the challenge.' In the video he says, 'I found that all the time I was here, behind that challenge, there was a love and kindness that made it very special to be Trinity's pastor.' So "here" he remained until he retired in 1994. His sermons and radical adherence to his calling stirred his congregation to the point that many would come rolling into the parking lot on Sunday mornings from vacations or wherever so as not to miss a sermon. He instituted a Christmas Eve service for Charlotteans that ran from 11:00pm until Christmas morn was ushered in at 12:00 midnight, and it was the hottest seat in town for years, with standing-room-only crowds of adults coming from family dinners and Christmas toasts to hear Lou deliver his sermon and to hear the Trinity Choir under the direction of Carolyn Darr deliver the message of Jesus's birth and what it could mean for 20th century people.

Along the way, starting in 1973, he began a yearly retreat to Montreat, NC, and on that 3rd weekend in October of every year, the church closed its doors in Charlotte (unheard of!) and headed for the hills literally to hear the best theologians and writers of the day. He convinced Tony Abbott, Frederick Buechner, Walter Brueggemann, Samuel Terrien, Will Willimon, Bishop John Spong, Diogenes Allen, and many others to come and lecture. Lou had the Trinity members reading the works of these writers in prelude, and so the attendees were ready to listen and to dialogue with the speakers, with many of the sessions informally going into the late-night hours. Anything was possible in these dialogues; any topic could be broached. I started attending Montreat retreats in 1976, rarely missing a year, and I often got the impression from the speakers that they looked at us, the congregants of Trinity Presbyterian Church, and asked themselves, 'who are these lay people who love to study the Word of God to such a depth?' I would answer today that we had a minister who was willing to take us to those depths.

During his early days in 1960s Charlotte, the Civil Rights movement took front-page attention. Lou Patrick preached that Trinity's doors would of course be open to anybody who entered— black or white. Anybody. He once said to me, "I drove away about $350,000 in pledges that year" because so

24

many influential and tithing congregants left. And then one night in the 1960s, Lou and Elizabeth's teenage daughters were at home with some of their friends visiting when a cross was burned in their front yard because of Lou's stand on integration in those early integration days. He was called to follow the voice of God's calling, the deep calling unto deep. All his yesterdays and all his tomorrows were gathered into these moments.

When I joined Trinity Presbyterian Church in 1976, I was a 26-year-old just starting my adult life after college. I worked at The Intimate Bookshop in Charlotte for a while, because as an English major in college, just being around books felt like home. My best friend at the shop was Katie Early, a female in the first class of females at Davidson College. Katie was a friend of Tony Abbott, the English professor there, and she even lived with the Abbotts for a time. Then I entered the Masters of Arts program at the University of North Carolina at Charlotte. I mention all this because as a person nurtured by words already, I found the atmosphere at Trinity in some ways like a university, a place where ideas and study and classes and fellowship surrounded me. My friend Katie spoke often of the Abbotts, and I also heard of Tony Abbott through Lou Patrick and Trinity. Lou invited Tony to come to Trinity and give lectures on poets and poetry. After one such evening, Lou wrote this thank-you to Tony:

"The last three nights brought a new high tide into our church's life. You found us on Dover Beach and left us looking forward to swinging on Birches.

Even if we could have found for ourselves the material you shared with us, the secret ingredient would have been missing; i.e., your gracious way of sharing it. It was your "feel" that quickened our feelings and turned the three nights into one shining epiphany."

Lou seemed to have established a church home for the arts, a place that opened windows upon the human condition even as he opened windows to show us the One we praised through scripture and song in the space called Trinity Presbyterian Church. Lou and Tony Abbott remained friends for all of Lou's life.

It probably must be said that Lou Patrick's calling must have been hard on his family. His writing late into the night on weekends in his study, the early morning memorization of his sermons so that he rarely had to take a manuscript into the pulpit, the devotion to the Word of God that precluded many other words like "family." His family, living in the manse on the Trinity property, probably paid a price for his time in his study. The light in that study seemed to be on at all hours, and congregants and friends and referred strangers knew they could call and slip in the back door that led to that study with the light on. From Providence Road, a major Charlotte thoroughfare, one could look at the church and see his car parked outside his study door. The beneficiary of Lou's calling was The World, not necessarily his family. Still, years later when Lou was near death, his daughter Jane said, "People always talk about Dr. Patrick this or Dr. Patrick that . . . but he was just 'Dad' to me." That seemed to be enough for Jane. Was it enough? Who's to say.

In the early days at Trinity, Lou took opportunities to travel to conferences to learn and study the works of current theologians. It was on one of these sabbaticals that Lou Patrick heard about an ordained Presbyterian minister and writer named Frederick Buechner; afterward, he began introducing the members of the congregation to Buechner's works. Lou enlisted Goldie Stribling, Betty McLaney and ultimately Tony Abbott to help frame a reading of Buechner's words from his *The Alphabet of Grace* for the 1973 Montreat Retreat. It was successful, so much so that Tony Abbott used the presentation at Davidson soon after. Also, thereafter, the relationship between Fred Buechner's writings and the Charlotte community became so symbiotic that at one time in those decades more Fred Buechner books were sold in the Charlotte, NC, region than in any other area of the country. One winter's day in the early 1970s, Goldie Stribling read an advertisement in *The Christian Century* magazine about a lecture taking place in January in Bangor, Maine, with Frederick Buechner as guest speaker. Goldie said to her friend Lou, "You'd be chicken not to go!" And so, Lou went on that dare, taking with him a leather pouch prepared by Goldie and Betty McLaney and filled with the same items Native American Herman Redpath carried around his neck in Frederick Buechner's 1974 novel *Lion Country*: a bird's wing, a box of Sunmaid raisins, a pocketknife, a few $10 bills of play Monopoly money. Lou flew to Bangor, and, in-between lectures, he saw Fred Buechner sitting in an anteroom. Lou walked by and heaved the leather pouch into the empty chair next to Buechner. Upon opening it, Buechner knew he needed to meet the man who went to the trouble of assembling the pouch (although Goldie Stribling and Betty McLaney had done the work!). Then and there began a friendship that lasted until Lou's death. What drew these two ordained Presbyterian ministers together? Fred Buechner has documented in many of his own writings the effects on his life of the death by suicide of his father when he was ten years old. Perhaps these two Presbyterian Ministers of the Word were drawn together because they shared a sense of loss with regard to their fathers. Perhaps it was because they shared the experience of being under the teachings of many of the same professors and writers because they both went to seminary. Maybe it was their shared sense of humor, and, because of it, they could laugh together when they were together, which was not often enough for either of them. Perhaps it was the shared belief that no matter how deep the darkness of the human condition could be, God was with them in that darkness, calling unto them as only deep can call unto deep. I think both of these men would say, like the young girl on the way to the guillotine, "I believe God sent you to me." That belief bound them, made the darkness a little less dark at that place where "Deep calls unto Deep." Fred and Lou both knew of deep loss, but they also felt the abiding love of God. They were not afraid of this calling from God, for they believed that humans cry "Out of the depths" just like the poet in Psalm 131. Fred dedicated his memoir *The Sacred Journey* to Lou. It reads, "For Louis Patrick and all the other saints, remembered and forgotten, along the way."(2) Fred Buechner and Lou Patrick each gave to the other an understanding. What was understood? That you have to stalk the gaps in the rock to find the mystery. That the reward of doing so brings light, not darkness. I found in Lou's files this quote from Albert Einstein: "The most beautiful thing we can experience is the mysterious. The man who can no longer pause to wonder, and stand rapt in awe, is as good as dead; his eyes are closed." After reading Annie Dillard's 1974 Pulitzer prize-winning book *Pilgrim at Tinker Creek*, and after introducing it to his parishioners, Lou used her words to underline and point to the Psalmist's mountain experience of the thunder of God's cataracts. He often used these words of Dillard:

"The gaps are the thing. The gaps are the spirits' one home, the altitudes and latitudes so dazzlingly spare and clean that the spirit can discover itself like a once-blind man unbound. The gaps are the clefts in the rock where you cower to see the back parts of God; they are the fissures between mountains and cells the wind lances through, the icy narrowing fiords splitting the cliffs of mystery. Go up into the gaps. If you can find them; they shift and vanish, too. Stalk the gaps."(3)

In a letter to me upon the death of my own father in 1999, Lou wrote to me in Silver Bay, New York, using words we had both read and studied.

Dearest Janet,

The restorative Adirondack airs of Silver Bay—like the healing waters of Golden Pond, the calming powers of Lake Placid, most of all Annie's [Dillard] Waters of Separation—are your invisible means of support. The world continues on its apparently indifferent and predetermined path, as though nothing earth-stopping has happened. And people, wearing their protective gear, go about their accustomed ways, as if mindless of significant loss. But inside your skin the bleeding goes on. The throes of grief still grip. Occasionally, even breathing comes hard. Yet, there is still the sparkle in the dew on the grass, the little green leaves in the wood, the wind on the water. And the world goes on, who knows why.

You have given us the awesome gift of letting us share in your sorrow. Blessed are the friends with whom we can laugh. Much more blessed— and rare—are the friends with whom we can weep. All of us are mortal and Death the Pawnbroker who already has our number. Is there love enough anywhere to redeem any and all of us?

May you find in the mercy of God, the grace of Christ, the comfort of the Holy Spirit your redemption.

Remember us who are stalking the gaps with you, sometimes falling, but always heading for Home.

Heart's love,   Lou

Imagine what it was like to receive not just mere words of condolence but the exact words I needed to hear. Imagine writers like Lou Patrick finding other writers who do not choose mere words but the exact words to match the deepest longings in himself to feel the closeness of God, to, with him, stalk the gaps, and like Einstein, stand with only the "Ahhh" of wonder on one's lips, because deep down, when deep calls unto deep, that's the response.

Probably the most asked for, the most replicated, sermon by Lou Patrick was one entitled, "The 'Ah' of Wonder." It was chosen by the editor Will Willimon for a book entitled *Sermons from the Duke Chapel* (2005) to join the sermons of other preachers at Duke University's Chapel. In Lou's September 30, 1984, sermon to the students at that " great towering church" in Durham, NC, he speaks of those moments when words fall short when describing the "wonder hidden deep-down inside" ordinary things, the moments when our breath is taken away and all we can manage is an "ah-h-h." But a lover of poetry of course knows that a poet will at least attempt to capture a little of the wonder, that even though the moment is past, there is a desire to share something of it.

Lou Patrick tries to capture some of that wonder in his sermon at Duke Chapel, hoping that the students might pause and ponder the hiddenness of deep-down things, for, like the Psalmist, Lou thinks that one encounters the God of the deep at those moments. This sermon, however, does not dwell on the sufferings of humans per se, but on the courage to "see" not with the eyes but through the eyes. Of course, the sufferings are implied. Lou uses the story of Jacob to illustrate the 'ah' of wonder; Jacob, that young man in Scripture on the run for his life, who rests his head, and, instead of bad dreams, is given a beautiful dream from God. What Lou wanted the Duke young people to see is that Jacob had an 'ah' moment when he woke. Jacob uttered these words: "Surely the Lord was in this place and I knew it not." Deep down, deep in his dream, God was calling unto him. Lou goes on to say: "All this "ah" in the midst of everyday things . . . The earth is the place of thy glory. That's why this chapel—to remind us of nothing more than that. Not that He's in the chapel, but all the glory that is *here* comes from *There*. Or we would not be here ourselves. How else can you say it? Lick a finger and feel the now."(4)

Lou packs the sermon with ways to see better, opening as many windows as possible. He quotes Tennyson, he quotes C.S. Lewis, he uses the words of Annie Dillard, he uses Alyce Walker, he even imagines God talking to us. Lou has God say, "For astonishment is that in which I delight. These who can stand before an everyday event and say, 'this is the Lord's doing,' that is marvelous in my eyes!"(5)

Lou ends the sermon with the C.S. Lewis poem "The Late Passenger," and therein is an example of readers being lifted up by a sadness, in this case the sadness that Noah's Ark sailed without the unicorn. The unicorn reflects the wonder of creation and a Christ-like uniqueness, and when the sons of

Noah do not let the creature in when he comes late and knocks
on the door of the ark, Noah says:

"Look, look, it would not wait,
it turns away; it takes its flight. . .
Oh, noble and unmated beast.
My sons were all unkind.
On such a night what stable and what manger
Will you find?
Oh, those hoofs; oh, cataracts of mane;
Now what furrows shall be plowed
Across the hearts of men
Before it comes to stable
And to manger once again?
And all the world may curse the hour
When you were born.
Because of you, the ark must sail
Without the unicorn".

Lou asked, "Have you seen a unicorn lately?" He says they are
gifts that come to us in our daily walks, "For holy holy, holy,
Lord God Almighty, the Earth is the place of thy glory."(6)

Lou and C.S. Lewis, and all the writers that try to tell us of the
"deep-down-ness of things" entreat us not to be afraid to
journey to the deepness, into the gaps, for there, wonder of
wonders, will God be found, and if we feel the wonder, Lou
says, by it "we are being borne aloft even in the now." When
one enters the realm of the deep, whether the cataracts of mane

on the unicorn which C.S. Lewis compares to the wonder of the Christ born into a stable, or the wonder of God's cataracts and its sounds that billow over us, God tells us "be not afraid, for I am with you." Were the listeners that day in the Duke Chapel borne aloft by the good news Lou came to preach, even after the listeners enter some of the deep sadnesses of life?

I never heard Lou say anything concerning his sermon being included in the book *Sermons from Duke Chapel* with such illustrious sermons by his peers, but surely it was gratifying, he who had given all his yesterdays and his tomorrows for this calling to preach "Deep calls unto deep" which ends in the good news of "The 'Ah' of Wonder," of God with us on this earth.

I do know, however, that when he and I compared our thoughts on Kazuo Ishiguro's *The Remains of The Day* published in 1989, that novel that examines a character's coming to terms with his past career, past choices, and what remains in the twilight of his life, I sensed some darkness clouding Lou's life as he faced retirement from Trinity. Like the main character in Ishiguro's novel, Lou may have been looking inwardly and backwardly at his life, maybe thinking of the things left undone or unattended. Lou never reconciled with his father, even though his father lived in South Carolina with his 'other family' until his death at 84 in 1981. Fred Buechner had encouraged Lou to see his father before his father died, thinking of the possibility of that event for which he himself never had an opportunity with his own father. He wrote to Lou about this in March of 1981, and after including a response to a few things Lou had written to him, Fred says, "And [about] your feeling that you must now go see your father while he's still around, I can't help feeling that if you do, there will be much healing in it for you both. But the enormous risk and difficulty of it doesn't escape me either. It's almost as if somebody were to tell me I could go see my father." But Lou did not go or could not go. In Lou's files kept at Trinity for years after his death, I came across this letter Lou wrote to Dr. Erskine Clarke on May 2, 1972:

Dear Dr. Clarke:

Thank you for the time and thought you have devoted to my father and to his well-being.

For more than a quarter of a century he and I have traveled in totally unrelated orbits. The need for any reconciliation between us because of 'bitter memories' and 'deep wounds' does not exist because those resentments do not exist. Out of practical necessity we have lived in separate worlds. I am a stranger to his present family and would be an intruder in their lives.

If my father believes I have any ill will towards him, you may safely reassure him that such is not so. Both he and his present family have my best thoughts and sympathetic concern. I hope that they will understand that I remain an 'outsider' because I believe that is my best contribution to their happiness.

Thank you again for your dedicated pastoral ministry to my father. I am very glad to know that he has you for his spiritual counselor.

Gratefully Yours,
H. Louis Patrick

It is hard to say whether this response was a caring and sacrificial response Lou would have possibly counselled anyone to make who was in the same situation, or whether his staying away was a result of not letting the buried pain come to the surface. I can only guess that it was a bit of both. Lou's friend Fred Buechner says in the introduction to *Telling Secrets,* "I have come to believe that by and large the human family all has the same secrets . . .They are telling in the sense that they tell what is perhaps the central paradox of our condition—that what we hunger for perhaps more than anything else is to be known in our full humanness, and yet that is often just what we also fear more than anything else."(7) Could Lou not bring himself to enter that place where secrets are buried? Fred had encouraged him to go see his father, that by "entering that deep place inside us where our secrets are kept that we come perhaps closer than we do anywhere else to the One. . ." I am reminded of the complex family relationships borne by the characters in Shakespeare's *King Lear,* for the old king came too late to the foibles humans all carry, came to realize too late there are things that can't be rectified. Is it too close a comparison for me to say that when I read *King Lear,* which I have done through the years since studying it as a young woman, I picture Lear and see Lou? I don't mean in a too-close comparison of their lives, but in a relative way, as older powerful men coming to grips with that very fact.

After his retirement in 1994, Lou's home study (the manse garage was turned into a large beautiful book-lined study with its own outside entrance designed by architect and friend Bonson Hobson) became a place for weekly poetry readings by a small number of us who wished to read and, above all, to hear him read in that South Carolina-accented bass voice the words of poetry. Over that last decade of Lou's life, we few who attended read books of poetry aloud because poetry was food to him—and us. His friend Tony Abbott was a source. Tony and Lou's relationship was a lasting one, born of an abiding faith in the Divine found in the "deep-down-ness" of things and a commonality of ideas and writers.

Tony Abbott became an illustrious poet and novelist in his own right through the years; he was the crackerjack teacher of English at Davidson College who could track down for Lou those poetry anthologies like Editor David Impastato's *Upholding Mystery*, Editor David Curzon's *The Gospels in Our Image, and* Editor Czeslaw Milosz's *Book of Luminous Things*. In Lou's home study that smelled of tobacco and strong coffee, about ten of us read hundreds and hundreds of poems by writers who strived for the right words rather than just mere words. These poems were written by the best the world's writers had to offer, and the poets came from the world over: Denise Levertov, Wendell Berry, Daniel Berrigan, Louise Erdrich, Li-young Lee, Mary Oliver, Wislawa Szymborska,

Robert Hass, Li Po, Gunnar Ekelof, Joseph Brodsky, Raymond Carver, Seamus Heaney, and so many more. In the poet Milosz's words, explaining a bit about poetry, he says, "When the Japanese poet Basho advised a poet describing a pine to learn from the pine, he wanted to say that contemplation of a thing—a reverent and pious approach to it—is a prerequisite of true art." When Lou used such an idea, not to talk about art but about the Divine, he often chose "Flower in the Crannied Wall" by Alfred, Lord Tennyson. I couldn't begin to say how many times he quoted this poem in sermons, in talking. He used it in the sermon at Duke Chapel. He loved it like scripture.

"Flower in the crannied wall
I pluck you out of the crannies.
I hold you here, root and all, in my hand,
Little flower—but if I could understand
What you are, root and all, and all in all,
I should know why God and man is."

During those last days of his preaching and teaching at Trinity and the decade of classes in his home study, Lou took many opportunities to actually go to hear poetry readings by the leading poets of the day. He took in Mary Oliver and David Whyte at Pease Auditorium at Central Piedmont Community College in Charlotte where Irene Honeycutt brought poets for a Literary Festival every spring. He listened to Czeslaw Milosz at UNC-Charlotte and turned to me and said, "I have never heard such spare and clear poems. He writes directly of God." Lou knew that Milosz was writing about the gaps and encountering the Divine.

Lou and I attend the David Whyte poetry reading in Pease Auditorium at Central Piedmont Community College.

But the cloud I referred to earlier that seemed part of the discussion Lou and I had about *The Remains of the Day*, the remains of *his* days, may have been brought on by the fact that Lou himself was not preaching any longer. He was not choosing his own words and the words of others, ordering them and preaching them. Sharing them. I also know that he had hoped at one time to write a book of sorts on the French existentialist Albert Camus, but he just couldn't get it done. Perhaps he knew his health was not robust, that his days for being the Whale-tale Preacher of the past were closing fast.

For these and maybe a hundred more reasons, he said this to me about those "remains of the day" in his own life: "It's not enough." I have no remembrance of my exact response to this. I hope I tried to convince him that what he had given to me, to his parishioners, to the everyday people *and* the famous people he had met along the way was wonderful, meaning full of wonder. I tried to tell him that he was *still* giving words to these deepest of longings and what it means to be human and what it means to seek God in the gaps with those who gathered in his study. Who knows how I worded it. But I was trying to convince him that there *is* worth in the remains of the day. He looked at me with his sleepy-eyed grin and said no more. He had cried out from his deepest feelings. What more can any of us do?

Lou Patrick's life testifies to that destiny he spoke of early in his sermons. The Whale-tale Preacher of Doris Betts's childhood stayed larger than life for all his days. He had put his yesterdays and tomorrows in the belief that the deep-down-ness of things would bring joy along with sadnesses. In his remaining days, even when his health failed in some ways, his back having a hard time holding the weight of him without pain, he never faltered in his belief in God. When 9/11 came with its horrific crashes on that Tuesday, the same day as his poetry class in his study, we few were together when we heard about the first plane crashing into the tower. Turning on Lou's tv, we collectively gasped when we watched the second plane hit the second tower. Unlike most people in the world, Lou didn't leave the tv on, didn't keep replaying the images that morning. He switched it off and offered a prayer. He read a couple of poems and then urged us to go home. I wish I could remember some of his prayer, some of the poetry. But our minds were too numb to remember much besides the images we had seen together. What I do know, though, is that Lou turned off the images of this world, of bedlam, and turned to the God he knew was there in the deep sadness with us. "Deep calls unto deep at the thunder of His cataracts," and Lou believed that that thunder overcame the thunder of those planes. Could he prove it? Of course not, but he had chosen years before to put all his eggs in that basket of hope. That we could be comforted even in the deep, because that is where we meet God. That big man, driving around his world in that big car with a cigar between his lips and a halo of smoke around his head, careened around corners with his faith in that God who called him from the deep and who led him through all the joys and the sorrows that "billowed over him." Excerpts from that dialogue from 1996:

41

Lou—I'm trying to get to that place for which I was made because I remember. I remember that place for where I have yet to be. I've got this idea of home in me because of the place and the time when I really was at home the way only a child can be at home.

Janet—What would you say to the person who is too at home? We like *The Wizard of Oz* because she clicks her heels and says, 'there's no place like home' and she got to go home.

Lou— No! What she was always saying was "I don't believe this is Kansas. She wanted to get back to a place where she'd never been.

Janet—Yes, and there's no place like home. I want to go home, too.

Lou—There 's no place like home. We all have a longing to get home, but we're talking about a home that is not available in terms of being a child again. It's not available in terms of being in the same place anymore than we can be in the same time anymore. [T.S.] Eliot said it's to get back to the beginning and understand it for the first time—what home is. What we've been calling home all this time. It's something for which we only have hints and glimpses. But we know we are homesick. Deep down, any night we sit out and look at the stars, we either get this feeling we are in an alien universe or of being on our way to something we have not yet seen or heard, to something that has not yet entered into our understanding.

Janet—This sounds like an idea in Wordsworth's poetry that the child is father of the man.

Lou—I think in a real sense the only person who has ever lived in this world at home . . . was Jesus. He is the only one I know who could say, "This is my Father's world."

At the end of this exchange, Lou quotes a poem by Jessica Powers:

Everything Rushes, Rushes

"The brisk blue morning whisked in with a thought:
everything in creation rushes, rushes
toward God—tall trees, small bushes,
quick birds and fish, the beetles, round as naught,

eels in the water, deer on forest floor,
what sits in trees, what burrows underground,
what wriggles to declare life must abound,
and we, the spearhead that run on before,

and lesser things to which life cannot come:
our work, our words that move toward the Unmoved,
whatever can be touched, used, handled, loved —
all, all are rushing on *ad terminum*.

So I, with eager voice and news-flushed face,
cry to those caught in comas, stupors, sleeping;
come, everything is running

flying,
leaping,
hurtling through time!
And we are in this race!"(8)

In this poem, everything in creation is rushing to God. The 'everything' forms a list, one thing after another. The point, may I say it, is that often humans want to stay in this human race for mortal longings of *this* world. But that lends itself to just "partly living," to quote Eliot again. That leads to the thunder of our own voices, not God's. This race that we are in means we are heading for home. Lou liked this poem that echoed his lifetime of preaching about our true home with Him, the one to which God is calling to us with a thunderous call from the deep.

Lou may have said "It's not enough" when asked about the remains of his days, but as one who heard these words come from deep down inside him, I am convinced that even that deep sadness did not keep him from hearing the good news, from choosing the exact words to share, to choose the old and new poetry of those who also care about the exact word that makes the difference. One who is journeying on, like the poet Wendell Berry who says in his poem " I move in the descent / of days from what was dreamed / to what remains. / In the stillness of this single place / where I'm resigned to die / I'm not free of journeys: / one eye watches while the other sleeps."(9)

The last time I spoke with Lou, he was in Presbyterian Hospital, and even though we had reason to believe he would recover, his body took a turn for the worse and he died there within the week. He was in pain when I stood by his bedside, and perhaps I shouldn't have, but I quoted something that I hoped would make him smile. I had found a prayer in one of my family histories about the Scottish Presbyterians who settled in the Blue Ridge Mountains of North Carolina. A Methodist minster said that he had never met such stubborn people as evidenced by this Presbyterian minister's prayer that goes like this: Oh Lord, help me always to be right, for Thou knowest how hard I am to turn." Even in the pain, even *through* the pain, Lou laughed.

And now that Lou is journeying on from his death in 2006, I smile to imagine that when Lou met his Lord face to face on his journey from glory to glory, God said "You *were* right." May he know that he left with us who remain enough words to last us until *we* journey on, words that speak of being found in this mortal life by the God who is with us in the through-bearing and who finally bears us aloft in joy.

Anthony S. Abbott

"And your very flesh shall be a great poem." —from Leaves of Grass
by Walt Whitman

"When I was nine years old, my family dissolved. It was the single most traumatic event of my life." So starts an interview with Tony Abbott in 2015. What happened was the firing of a rifle by his mother which hit Tony's stepfather in the shoulder, which led to the police coming, which led to the family dissolving. His stepfather went to New York City to live. His mother went to the hospital. Tony said, "What do you do with a nine-year-old after that? You send him to boarding school," and there, as he wrote later in life in a poem about himself as that boy, he "put his tears away in the pocket with his used handkerchief."

And so began the events in the life of Anthony 'Tony' Abbott that laid the foundation for all the words that were to come from his pen, from that place deep within him where "deep calls unto deep." Like Lou Patrick pouring himself into sermons, Tony Abbott took his childhood and the succeeding years and poured them into his writings. *We* are the recipients of that gift.

Born in San Francisco in 1935 to Frances Hayden and Howard Johnson Abbott, Tony spent those first years of life on the West Coast with his parents and an older sister Nancy. From birth Tony suffered from bilateral club feet, and, after a number of corrective surgeries, he settled into the limp he kept always. Those feet of his were a source of self-consciousness and unease for many years, a topic he spoke to in his writing. His sister Nancy was nine years his senior, and as the marriage of his parents foundered, he and his sister left the West Coast with his mother to live on the East Coast near her family. His parents divorced and his mother married again, this time to William (Bill) Covington, the stepfather in the aforementioned shooting. Then comes the summer of Tony's ninth year, and the drinking life of his mother, the firing of that rifle, and the boarding schools thereafter.

Much later in life, Tony Abbott wrote about these early days of his life, channeling them into poetry and into fiction in two novels. For years, he buried his tears and emotions, figuring out how to handle the loss of home. For years he stayed most of the year at boarding schools, but there was always the question of where to go during vacations. He was never quite sure where he would be staying. He called New York City his "base of operation;" his mother lived there in a hotel when she was released from the hospital after treatment for her alcoholism. His stepfather Bill lived there, and, even after the shooting incident, Tony sometimes stayed with him. And his sister married and lived there with her husband Leonard Gordon. Like Lou Patrick, Tony lost his childhood home and was thrown, often, on his own resources. The first school he was sent to was The Fay School in Southborough, MA. Nine years old with feet that had to be massaged morning and night and then fitted into special shoes, he learned the ropes and found at the school a place of safety and stability, a place of caring teachers. In his second year at Fay, when he earned a weekend away from school, he wrote to his mother that he was coming, and he took the train to New York City to meet her; he entered Grand Central Station only to find no mother there. He waited. He panicked. He tried to keep his tears hidden but they came anyway. Then he remembered he could call his sister Nancy, and she came, explaining how sick his mother was. Nancy—she would come to his aid over and over again through his life. Tony retold that abandonment event in the poem "In Grand Central Station" published in his 2011 book *If Words Could Save Us.*

". . . He has watched
for his mother's blue coat with the torn hem
and the white scarf she wears on rainy days.

He is starting to cry and he does not like
to cry at all. . . He wipes his eyes
With his handkerchief, and then he feels
for the first time the icy touch of death.

She will not come at all. She will never
come . . . He stands, puts his tears away
in the pocket with his used handkerchief."(10)

Tony also wrote of that day in Grand Central (and what it did to him) through the character David Lear in his semi-autobiographical novel *Leaving Maggie Hope* published in 2003.

"He would not cry like that again. He would not need like that again. He would be strong. He would take care of himself."(11) This steely resolve characterized the early life of Tony Abbott, and probably mirrors the plight of many children who experience a loss of home. In the poem "The Boy from Somewhere Else," published in 2020, Tony describes this feeling in himself. "But there was in his voice/ the deep well of absence./ . . He would find one day the person/ who could hear his music./ When she came, he would recognize her/ at once—as one knows the coming storm/ by the first, distant clap of thunder".(12) There it is, that recognition of love for which we all wait in some form or other. In this poem, Tony wrote for the child within himself still, addressing the deep well of absence while also listening for the thunder of love. It is reminiscent of the poet in Psalm 42 yearning for God's thundering cataracts to billow over him as deep calls unto deep. It is out of this sense of the deep-down-ness of things, the dark times that humans face, that Tony Abbott writes about later as an adult. His gift to his readers, however, is that no matter how dark life gets, there is also the light of hope.

And what else, besides Nancy and his own resilience, came to his aid through those early years? One other aid was the financial aid his godmother sent, the godmother he didn't even know he had! Marion Lowe was a dear friend of his parents back when they were all young in California. At the Fay School, Tony had wondered who paid for this expensive schooling, and for years assumed it was his stepfather Bill. The surprise that he had never been told about Marion Lowe may be astounding to us who have a home in which to ask such questions, but for Tony, the unanswered questions just continued his off-balance existence when he was not at school. Marion Lowe was generous with her wealth, thank goodness, and paid for his tuition for school and other necessities, but she stayed in the background of his life, just like his real father Howard Johnson Abbott. Marion always hoped his real family would re-emerge as a unifying force in his life. It didn't happen that way. Tony remained unable to help his mother; after all, he was a child coping with an alcoholic mother. He also remained unable to blend in with his father's new family, not being able to be himself. Fred Buechner writes in his book *Longing For Home,,* "there lies the longing to know and be known by another fully and humanly, and that beneath that there lies a longing, closer to the heart of the matter still, which is the longing to be at long last where you fully belong." If that is true, and I believe it is, how hard it is when we are not seen, not known, not able to find a home.

Besides the aid from his sister Nancy and his godmother Marion Lowe, Tony found another source of aid. Words. Words would come to aid him in the place he felt safest . . . school. In the performances of plays at school, in the writing he did for classes, and in the words of support from teachers, he found enough aid to see him through those days. Tony gives the English Teacher Mrs. Benzaquin these lines in *Leaving Maggie Hope*: "Every word is a miracle, boys. Don't forget that". (14) Tony Abbott never did.

Whenever Tony found himself wrestling with that darkness of things, the uncertainties of the hand he had been dealt as a child, his homelessness that he couldn't seem to rectify, he also found a way to the light, particularly with help from teachers. "Among all the things I've admired about Tony Abbott's work over the years—and those things are legion—his refusal to flinch or shy away from his spiritual preoccupations intrigues and thrills me most profoundly" says poet Joseph Bashanti in his praise for Tony's book *The Angel Dialogues*.(15) Where did this exploration of the spiritual come from? Unlike Lou Patrick who began his life in a religious community, Tony's family was neither church-going nor spiritual. And yet.

For his spiritual journey, Tony tells me in an interview, "My oldest possession is a Bible (KJV) my mother gave me for my ninth birthday, which was before I was sent to boarding school in September of my ninth year. I took the Bible with me. Don't know where the desire for a Bible came from, but it was there . . . I have notes in the Bible (I wrote in it!) taken during Sunday school class at Fay School." But after this sentence, he gives much of the credit for his spiritual underpinnings to the Headmaster at Kent School, his private high school in Connecticut where he went after Fay School. Besides being Headmaster, the Rev. John O. Patterson preached powerfully and became a forever-influencer in Tony's life. Patterson is thinly disguised as Father Perkins in *The Three Great Secret Things*. Here is how Tony portrayed him in that novel and his influence on the character David Lear:

51

"Every Sunday morning, he preached to them from the high stone pulpit. . . The other services were short, mostly hymns and prayers, beautiful prayers with words that David learned easily. 'O Lord, support us all day long, until the shadows lengthen, and the evening comes, and the busy world is hushed, and the fever of life is over, and our work is done. Then in thy mercy, grant us a safe lodging, and a holy rest, and peace at the last.' The first time he heard Father Perkins speak those words, he felt his throat catch and his heart stir. He loved 'shadows lengthen' and 'busy world is hushed''. The words sounded like what they said. . . And to explain Christ to the boys, Father Perkins told them, "Every evening here in this chapel we bring to God the concerns of the day. Every Sunday we bring to this chapel the work we have done during the week. We bring everything we have done during the week to Christ—our studies, our sports, our jobs— to remind ourselves that without His blessing there is no meaning to these activities. In the form of bread and wine, we carry these activities from the back of this chapel to the altar, where God blesses them and gives them back to us.'"(16)

That catch in the throat, that belief in the blessings of God, echo the haunted-ness of Lou Patrick when he heard Psalm 42. That deep calling, that place where you feel and hear the calling and meet the Divine made sense to Lou Patrick. It made sense to Tony Abbott as a boy, and Tony lived out of that stirring in his heart forever after, later capturing some of those feelings in poems like "Noli Me Tangere" about the resurrection of Jesus, "The Christmas Celebration" about the birth of Jesus and Jesus's crucifixion, "To Have Been There" from John 6:40, all of these in his last book *The Dark Side of North*. Actually, these feelings of such Divine moments are everywhere in Tony's works.

Tony Abbott continued to find his place in the world of academia. In 1950, while he was a sophomore at Kent, his secondary school, his mother and his grandmother died within months of each other. He says this about them in an interview years later: "They were so symbiotic in life (my mother being an only child) that it seemed ironically fitting that one could not live without the other. Both of them had drinking problems, and they both died finally from cancer." In his later poem "Dust Beneath My Shoe," from his book *A Small Thing Like a Breath*, he speaks of this time, this separate-ness from his real family. His tears stayed buried deep within him, but he began to cultivate resources within himself for the "through-bearing" Lou Patrick mentioned. He excelled at school, storing up words from teachers and from poets and writers he studied. He also excelled at sports and had an easy camaraderie with friends. After the Fay School and Kent School, Tony attended Princeton University, where he majored in English but took enough religion courses to minor in that discipline. His thesis for his MA at Princeton was "Shaw and Christianity," a variant of which he used for his dissertation at Harvard later on. He seemed to have always known that he would be a teacher, much like Lou Patrick knew he would be a preacher. As Tony himself said in an interview, "My soul is the soul of a teacher." In the recent September 2020 conversation I had with Tony, he listed for me some of his favorite poets:

> *"Start with Whitman....He says it all and says it wonderfully. When John Kennedy was assassinated, I read "When Lilacs Last in the Dooryard Bloom'd" to my English classes and let them go. My favorite Whitman poem is "Out of the Cradle Endlessly Rocking," a virtually perfect poem in its passion and in its music. There are several virtually astonishing sections of "Song of Myself." Whitman had the courage to say the things that were true which others were afraid to say. He and Emily Dickinson are our greatest American poets---totally different, but both geniuses each in his/her own way. If you asked me what my favorite poem is, I would say "The Love Song of J. Alfred Prufrock," which is really Eliot's masterpiece. I find myself quoting it all the time. "I grow old, I grow old, I shall wear the bottom of my trousers rolled...." My other favorite poem is Yeats's "The Second Coming," probably the most quoted poem of the 20th century, and one which describes exactly where we are today...Yeats is a poet of great passion (look at "Easter 1916"--what a great poem), but the passion is always controlled by craft---he never just lays it on the page....Look at two extraordinary poems "Adam's Curse" and "Sailing to Byzantium" for the extraordinary use of craft---rhyme, meter, and the ability to make it sound natural."*

And then, as if he couldn't find a good place to stop, he said,

"And then there is Jane Kenyon. I would like someone to read "Let Evening Come" at my funeral. And of course, Keats. No one is really better than Keats. . . Is that enough?"

No, there was never enough. Never an end to the conversation about poetry and poets and writers in general as evidenced by the use of "and" in that list. And yes, Jane Kenyon's "Let Evening Come" was read at his memorial service in October of 2020.

So, after Princeton, after getting his doctorate at Harvard, after meeting and marrying Susan Dudley whom he met when they both worked one summer at a ranch out west, Tony began his teaching career, armed with all these favorite works, all these words.

In 1964, Tony Abbott took a position as an Associate Professor of English at Davidson College in Davidson, NC. He now had a place, a home that did not move. He, along with wife Susan and children David, Lyn, and Stephen, settled into life on a college campus. Settled, that is, until their lives changed irreparably the day after Easter 1968. Tony and Susan woke to find that their almost-four year-old daughter Lyn had died in the night. They learned that a massive swelling of the brain, a form of encephalitis, had caused her death. Tony says of that time, "I had no language to express what happened." Having put away his tears years ago, he had forgotten how to cry, to use tears as a way to get to something like grief, to get to something holy. I am reminded of Lou Patrick's words to me, "How blessed are the friends with whom we can laugh. How more blessed—and rare— are the ones with whom we can weep." But for Tony at that time, he had to learn again to cry, to take out the tears and see where they led him. Out of unbearable grief he began to write. He says about that time, "I had no language for grief." But something was there in the darkness with him, calling him as he bore the unbearable. He began to write poetry. Using his daughter Lyn as a muse, he found aid once again in words. Poetry, what he calls "the voice of the soul," began to pour out of him onto the page during the 1970s. He also had the joyful birth of his son Andrew. The poetry of others that he carried with him surely must have helped him as he began putting his own words of life on paper. He took lessons from writers John Irving, Tim O'Brien, and others at the writers' workshop at The Bread Loaf Writers' Conference in Vermont. He begins to write not "the poor-old-pitiful-me-poem" as he called it, but poems like "Words are the only fingers of the soul/words spoken and heard/written and received." He found solace in words, and in teaching, and in human beings; did he find solace in a God who the psalmist believes is calling to us from the deep? The words to express his tears began to come, but it took time. In 1980, a student in his freshman composition class at Davidson wore a yellow raincoat. He says she was lovely and smart and the age his daughter Lyn would have been. Tony began to imagine his daughter as a freshman at Davidson and he wrote:

"The Girl in the Yellow Raincoat"

waits on the sidewalk outside
my window. The flower in her hair
is wet. She stands very still

her eyes focused upward on some
object I cannot see. She does not
move, but she smiles . . . slightly.

Perhaps she plays the cello
and she is humming Bartok silently
making the bow ripple with her tongue

against her teeth. Or, maybe, she waits
for a bus to take her to her lover.
or she has read a letter from Paris

or Istanbul and she smells coffee
and chestnuts steam roasted and she
hears in the cobbled streets the cries

of vendors under the aged curves
of bridges. Perhaps she is just a girl
standing in the rain by a stone bench
in the early morning while the
street shines. It is nothing - - you argue.
Then, why do I weep, and why are there
splinters in my palms, and why do I

stand here, long, long after she is
gone?"(17)

It is no wonder that this poem won The NC Poetry Society
Award and no wonder that the cover of that first book of
poems *The Girl in the Yellow Raincoat* published in 1989 shows a
man standing at a window. Tony's words are stalking the gaps,
those spare places where we just might hear the thunder of
God's cataracts and not just the world's. Like the poet of Job,
like the sermons of Lou Patrick, like others who are plunged
into the deepest darkness of hurt and despair, he let the billows
roll over him and then determines to look at the world, both
inside himself and outside himself, and see better. Who writes
with such clarity? Who brings to the listeners' eyes tears of
recognition of truth in these words? One for whom the tears
finally fall with grief and one with courage enough to word it
and still stand. One who has heard the deep calling unto deep.
One who remembers.

"Up the Rabbit Hole or Oz Remembered"

1
Think of the whole thing in reverse - -
Dorothy whirling back from Oz
Onto the flat plains of Kansas saying
"Yes, Auntie Em, I do love you."
Think of Alice flying up the rabbit hole
Onto the green English grass.

Think of a winter's day
Alice before the mirror
Dorothy under the quilted spread
Winter is Kansas. Winter is England.
Back there it was MGM over the rainbow technicolor
It was smiles in the trees and letters
Under doors and brown bottles to make you grow

It was the twirl of a lion's tail
And witches wilting into water

2
We wait for the snow to melt. We wait
For the sun. We stumble into the unfamiliar
Sound of birds and the slant light of spring.

Alice searches in the grass for the rabbit hole.
The wheat of Kansas stands endless.
We cannot find our way back, choose our way
Back. We can only wait.

Does it hurt - - this time between?
Like death - - it hurts
Like ice on the bone
Like marrow scraped

But it is only the silence before . . .

The beginning."(18)

This poem from Tony's first book, *The Girl in the Yellow Raincoat* sounds like T.S. Eliot's lines from *Little Gidding:* "We shall not cease from exploration/And the end of all our exploring/Will be to arrive where we started/And know the place for the first time."(19) Eliot, that favorite poet of Tony and Lou Patrick, writes that we cannot find our way back to the laughter of children in the garden, but we *can* look at it through the eyes of memory, we could even go to the garden, and we can know it for the first time. This poem of Tony's is reminiscent of Lou's comments that what Dorothy in the *Wizard of Oz* kept saying was "I don't believe this is Kansas." Dorothy caught a glimpse of another home. Fred Buechner says it this way in his book *Telling the Truth:*

> "But we are also from somewhere else. We are from Oz, from Looking-Glass Land, from Narnia, and from Middle Earth. If with part of ourselves we are men and women of the world and share the sad unbeliefs of the world, with a deeper part still, the part where our best dreams come from, it is as if we were indeed born yesterday, or almost yesterday, because we are also all of us children still . . . neither the world we live in nor the world that lives in us can ever entirely be home again any more than it was home for Dorothy in the end either because in the Oz books that follow The Wizard, she keeps coming back again and again to Oz because Oz, not Kansas, is where her heart is."(20)

The writer Tony Abbott, like these other writers, gives us this good news, even though he gives us the hurt we feel in these between times of through-bearing.

How DID Tony Abbott hear about the works of Fred Buechner that gave him such pleasure, such hope? It was by meeting Lou Patrick, Goldie Stribling, and Betty McLaney in 1973, as they worked to present a reading of Buechner's *Alphabet of Grace* to the Trinity Congregation at Montreat Conference Center. Tony came on board to help them arrange Buechner's work for presentation. "Thank goodness we found Tony," says Goldie Stribling when asked, "because we didn't know what we were doing." The presentation was so powerful, the relationship so satisfactory on all sides, that friendships resulted among Lou, Goldie, Betty, and Tony.

Tony was invited to give a series of lectures on poetry at Trinity Presbyterian Church. It was after those lectures that Lou wrote in that letter he sent to Tony, "It was your "feel" [for the material] that quickened our feelings." Because of Lou and that Montreat experience in 1973, Tony discovered the works of Frederick Buechner, who, like Lou and himself, knew grief and darkness, knew homelessness. Fred's father died by suicide when Fred was ten years old, and like Lou Patrick and Tony, he buried that grief deep within, struggling for years to keep it hidden from the world—and from himself. As an adult, Fred Buechner began the hard work of grieving for his father; he shared his journey in his memoirs, both his 'bearing-through' experiences as well as his joys. In fact, he says that ultimately his whole life's work was a search for his father. When you meet someone who puts into words for you that darkness within and the ways you bore them, and who offers those words as gifts so that they help the hearer, you hang on for dear life, thank God. Fred Buechner found Lou Patrick; Lou found Tony Abbott, Tony found Fred Buechner, I found Tony Abbott—and on and on it goes.

Deep calls unto deep. It is sometimes recognized. Lou and Trinity Presbyterian Church asked Tony to give more readings and lectures through the years. He twice gave a three-day series called the Gilchrist Lectures at Trinity, once on the writings of Fred Buechner and another time on the book *Prayer for Owen Meany* by John Irving. Having discovered Fred Buechner, he

Betty McLaney, Tony Abbott, and Goldie Stribling in Trinity Presbyterian Church's parlor

continued to read Buechner's work and even taught a class at Davidson called "Three American Prophets: O'Conner, Buechner, and Percy." In a lecture at Trinity, Tony opened by reading an excerpt from Buechner's book *Open Heart,* in which Buechner tells us of a teacher teaching Shakespeare's *King Lear* to high school students. Tony reads the part where students attempt, in spite of themselves, to answer the question "What evidence do you find in Act Three for a significant change in Lear's character?" One student said, "he's gotten kinder." Another student quotes from the play where Lear says about the Fool, 'I have one part in my heart / That's sorry yet for thee,' and says that is the evidence that Lear has gotten kinder. And Laura Fleischman, who 'sat in the back row next to a good-looking basketball player named Carl West,' said, "Also, he says a prayer for people.' The excerpt ends with Buechner's recalling that one student says that *we* are the 'poor naked wretches' Lear is praying for. Buechner says:

"Maybe I just ascribed my own thoughts to them . . . Laura Fleischman in the fullness of her time. William Urquhart in his fatness. Greg Dixon with his pimples. Carl West handsome and bored with the knowledge that he could have any girl in that room. They were the poor naked wretches, and at least for the moment they knew they were."(21)

Tony finished the excerpt and chuckled and then said, "I tell my students who take this Buechner class with me that if they are *not* captured by this, then the class is not for them." We in the audience laughed with him. We were ourselves captured.

Tony was himself captivating. He was funny. He was intense. When I first heard Tony lecture, I recognized a teacher who opened windows for the listener. Isn't that what teachers attempt? To open as many windows as possible into what it means to be human?

In 2007, an English professor named Dale Brown became the Director of the Buechner Institute at King College in Bristol, TN. The institute's aim was to further the conversation of faith and culture, using the writings of Fred Buechner to begin the dialogue. Tony Abbott and I were each asked by Dale Brown to present a lecture for the institute's Buechner Fest in Charlotte in 2014. I presented a lecture on Buechner's *Son of Laughter*, the imaginative look at the biblical story of Jacob. Tony presented an engrossing look at the parallels between his life and the life of Fred Buechner. The parallels are indeed extraordinary. They were both looking for an earthly home of stability. They both attended boarding schools. They both graduated from Princeton. They both suffered great loss: Fred his father, Tony his daughter. They both found words to help the suffering, particularly leading them to a faith in God that was profound. They both became acclaimed writers. They both found Lou Patrick as a friend. They found each other.

In the writings of Lou Patrick, Tony Abbott, and Fred Buechner, there is a startling symmetry of recognition of the darknesses of life, the sharing of those with the God of the deep, and the shafts of light through the darkness that help bear the almost unbearable. And they share this light with the world. This quote of Fred Buechner in his book *The Magnificent Defeat*, seems to sum up the questions posed by these three writers:

"My question is this: Are there in us, in you and me now that recklessness of the loving heart, that wild courage, that crazy gladness in the face of darkness and death, that shuddering faithfulness unto the end of the world, through which the new things can come to pass?"(22)

In the book *The Girl in the Yellow Raincoat* published in 1989, Tony includes a poem entitled "Before Forty," and it ends like this:

"So you want a happy ending? I don't know
Much about that. I cry a lot these days.
Not for broken shoelaces or spilled beer,
But for Bach and the Beatles and for
Beauty where I find it. I sleep later,
Dream more, and write stuff like this."(23)

Does it hurt, this through-bearing of people like Tony Abbott, Lou Patrick, and Fred Buechner? Of course. But in answer to my question of hurt and whether it is 'too much,' Tony says in our conversation in September 2020, " It took time . . . but I guess what I want to say is that writing about my daughter opened up a whole new part of me that had been closed for a long time, and I felt really good about that . . . even excited about that . . . I began to write poems about my mother, my father, my classmates at school— I went back to the business of remembering. Art is a combination of remembering and imagination . . . you start by remembering and imbue it with imagination. Then the whole thing takes on new life. When I write about these sad things, I am not sad. I am more fully alive." How these words echo the poet in Psalm 42 who says "These things I remember,/as I pour out my soul;" how they echo Lou Patrick's "Balm in Gilead," and how they are reminiscent of Fred Buechner's question which ends with "That shuddering faithfulness even unto the end of the world through which the new things can come to pass." But in spite of this deep-down-ness of things, which might seem at first to be overly serious, there is a certain airy lightness of being about these three writers, too. Lou's sleepy-eyed grin invited laughter. He laughed often, trading old and current stories about the foibles of humans with anyone sitting across from him at his study desk. And Tony's eyes twinkled mischievously, like he knew something we don't, and he laughed along with his audience when he read and lectured. Fred Buechner's conversion experience centers around the word 'laughter'. In a *Reader's Digest* article of Fred's, he quotes Jesus who says, "Blessed are you who weep now, for you shall laugh." All three found themselves in each other's company now and then. Lou and Fred went back and forth between Charlotte and Vermont. Lou and Tony set up lectures and readings at Trinity and saw each other at poetry events in the Charlotte area. Tony had the experience of meeting Fred in Middlebury, Vermont, at the time his son Stephen Abbott was teaching math at Middlebury College. Fred invited him down to his home and Tony got to visit Fred's Library, The Magic Kingdom of books and memorabilia, which was a powerful experience for Tony. "Buechner showed my wife and me all his amazing possessions in that holy and magical space. And when I started teaching the course at Davidson, I invited him to come to Davidson, and he and his wonderful wife Judy, and their two dogs, stayed with us two nights on their drive home from Florida to Vermont; he preached the Sunday after Easter, and all you Trinity folk came up to hear him."

To be inspired by another writer's words lifts one in unimaginable ways. For a writer to be thus inspired means that the words are sometimes used and then passed on to even more readers. When Fred Buechner recounts in his memoir the sad days of losing his only brother Jamie to cancer, he includes the story of Jamie asking him to write out a prayer he could use in these last days of life. Fred wrote a prayer and sent it to Jamie; since then, it has been given a title: "Jamie's Prayer." Fred was told that this prayer was at his brother's bedside when he died. Tony Abbott, being moved by this prayer, used it as a topic in one of his poems.

JAMIE'S PRAYER

"*Dear Lord, bring me through darkness into light. Bring me through pain into peace. Bring me through death into life. Be with me wherever I go, and with everyone I love. In Christ's name I ask it. Amen.*"

For Frederick Buechner, its author

When I read the prayer to myself
out loud alone in my room, I felt
the tears come and I knew for the first
time in many months that I would be
all right, that I would find myself again

that the dry ghost of these withering
months would not win after all.

Later, at the meeting, I read the prayer
out loud to the assembled council and said
that it was my favorite prayer, that I had
typed it out to give to anyone who might want
to put it on their bedside table as Jamie had.

I read it slowly with some emotion,
then sat down. At the end of the meeting
no one came up to me. No one wanted
the prayer.

In my room, I took the copies I had made
and cut them into tiny pieces, hundreds
of tiny pieces. Then with both hands full
I hurled the pieces to the ceiling and watched
as they came swirling down, covering
my mending heart with their tiny letters.(24)

Tony's poem captures the bittersweet feelings of being lifted
up by words only to find that others are not so moved when

they are shared. It is the plight of a preacher or a teacher or a writer, I think, to sometimes be disappointed when some of the deepest and darkest places in the human heart don't find an echo in the hearts of others. It is bound to happen, of course, but that doesn't make it any easier to watch the faces of those un-moved! That poem by Tony captures for us all those human moments when we want to share what has helped heal us, hoping others will be healed as well.

Like Lou Patrick, whose sermons are published by The Protestant Hour and in *Sermons from Duke Chapel* but also reside in the hearts of those who heard him Sunday after Sunday, Tony Abbott's outpouring of work is accessible by a wide community. His poetry found light in many poetry journals (There arc 18 such journals listed in the beginning pages of *The Girl in the Yellow Raincoat*) before his poetry was gathered into his own books for publication. His novel *Leaving Maggie Hope* won the Novello Literary Award in 2003. He has led as president the organizations that surround and encourage writers: The North Carolina Poetry Society, the North Carolina Writers' Network, and the Charlotte Writers' Club. He is known particularly in Davidson, and when I think of the young lives (and the not so young lives of his adult students) he captivated by words and by his very being, well, the numbers are too great to count. But there is something else besides, something that must be addressed. As gregarious as Tony Abbott was as a teacher, there is also a sense of his being an outsider, for it is as an outsider that the poet finds the inner home carried within, the one which holds the deepest sense of himself. It is then that the poet writes to explore this deepness, usually in solitude.

The lives of these three men are intertwined in a miraculous way that is hard to characterize other than by saying they and their gifts of words are sent to us from God. And also, it must be said, all three men are delightful company.

Tony retired from teaching at Davidson in 2001, beginning an outpouring of writing that resulted in five books of poetry and two novels. In 2015, I heard Tony read from a new work of his called *The Angel Dialogues*. Poet Joseph Bathanti calls it "a beautiful, humane book that takes stunning chances." On the afternoon of a reading from this new book at Southminster Retirement Home, Tony's longtime friend Goldie Stribling and I introduced him and away he went, reading from this work about a cynical poet who needs a muse, and an angel who comes to his rescue—sort of. The angel's red flowing hair, sense of absurd style, and knowledge from beyond human knowing, stirs the poet, stirs his heart. She stays with him a year, and they have magical conversations about everything from Yeats to church suppers to eternal life. In the poem "The Angel Thinks of Music," the poet feels brave:

"What is God like?" I ask.

God is like music, she says.(25)

In the poem, she has the poet think of his favorite piece of music (it's Mozart, Piano Concerto No. 21, Second

Movement) and she has him play the notes in his head. He does. But then the poet, as poets do, writes in words what he is hearing.

"I count the notes in my high mind. Each finger a world, each note black or white perfect in the moment, then gone. Tears come like rain after long drought."(25)

Tears, again written about. Felt. And two pages later, in the poem "The Angel Speaks of Death," the poet accuses the angel of knowing about death but not sharing her knowledge with him. She says that she's not allowed to tell him about death. But actually she does give an answer of sorts.

The dogwood in the spring, she whispers, *just is, it does not think about its isness.*

"Its isness," I laugh. "Where on earth did you get that?"

I made it up, she says. *Just be,* she says softly. *Don't worry. Let God worry for you.*"(26)

Maybe Tony, like the poet, does let go and let God, in that fairly trite platitude we hear so much these days. I do know that even in the darkness of human existence, even through his own darkness, Tony Abbott brings us to hope, the light of the world. In his newest book of poetry, he starts with the title poem called "The Dark Side of North," written in the midst of the 2020 pandemic. It ends this way:

"So stop, whoever you are, and look around you.
Perhaps I will be here, perhaps not. I am, they say,
among the most vulnerable. This is my remembrance.
I cannot touch you except with broken words
(azaleas pink and white quiver in the breeze)

We wonder what there will be when we walk once more on the
open streets. What price the touch
of a friend, a grandchild? On Palm Sunday, the Pope spoke
alone to an empty St. Peter's Square. No cardinals
(the fingers of love beckon through the greening leaves)."(27)

True to a lifetime of responding to the deep that calls unto deep, which shines a light forward for all of us who read his words, and, in this poem in the parentheses, Tony does not stay in the darkness of this time, of any time, because love calls, and he hears its calling through the greening leaves of the "is-ness" of this world which this world cannot hold, for there is another. In "A Poem for My Daughter on Her Fiftieth Birthday," the love for his daughter Lyn still shines before him when he says, "And now you have gone . . . beyond that blue call/ to another heaven far beyond the blue call/ of this tired earthfolk. . . . they all tell us move on. Sweet Jesus move on/ to what? . . . And I, I still have my eye open for you."(28)

What forward, through-bearing lines.

Before one of his poems in this last best book of poems, Tony quotes T.S. Eliot: "Old Men Should be explorers." Eliot also wrote, " O voyagers, o seamen, you who came to port,/ and you whose bodies will bear the trials and judgements of the sea,/ or whatever event . . . not farewell but fare forward, voyagers."(29) In his final poem in *The Dark Side of North* called "Last," I know what Tony is writing about as he writes a litany of 'lasts' and seems to say, like Lou Patrick, that beholding the beauty of this created world and those we love in it would mean never having enough. It is elegiac like so many of Tony's poems. But he knows that he is moving on like I am moving on, like everyone is moving on, Sweet Jesus. He knows, surely he knows, that the love of God and the love of humans combined in the words he has left for us, showing the 'is-ness' of things dark and light, are too wonderful for us. I am convinced, that wherever he's going, he carries those he loves with him, too. Fare forward, Tony Abbott.

Frederick Buechner

Elizabeth Patrick, Goldie Stribling, and I formed a group in 1997 called The Laughing Club. We met in the coffee shop within Borders Book Store in Charlotte, and our group's purpose was to drink coffee and laugh. We even had a motto—actually two! *She who laughs lasts.* The other was *And the laugh shall be first.* Goldie and I came up with the group in order to get Elizabeth out of the house once a week. Since her husband Lou Patrick's retirement, they were much together. We all know that breaks are good, as is laughter with friends. For years the three of us met on those Tuesday afternoons, for years I documented some of our 'doings' in that coffee shop, which sometimes led to entertaining others. One of our ways of entertaining (ways contrived to get what we wanted, which was laughter), was to make the visitors answer the questions James Lipton would ask his famous guests on the tv series "Inside the Actors Studio." One of the questions always asked was, "What is your favorite word?" On April 19, 1998, during one of the occasions when Fred and Judy Buechner passed through Charlotte and stayed with friends Lou and Elizabeth Patrick, the four of them plus Goldie and Bruce Stribling and Janet and Dale Sarjeant met for dinner at Providence Cafe. We three Laughing Club members, Elizabeth, Goldie, and Janet, talked about the Lipton questions and then asked Fred and Judy just the one question of their favorite word. Judy said, 'snow,' and Fred said, 'twilight.' My husband decided to give his: 'dinner,'

74

he said. What happened next? You got it—great laughter and dinner.

The life of the writer/theologian Frederick Buechner is as well-known to his readers as Tony Abbott's is to his readers and Lou Patrick to his parishioners. Tony Abbott and Fred Buechner are believers in the power of words to connect human beings to each other and to God, believing that if they tell their own life stories, it could open the possibility that hearers of these stories might believe that they are "not just journeys through time but as sacred journeys," and the assumption "that the story of any one of us is in some measure the story of us all,"(30) to quote Fred Buechner. Lou Patrick also believed in the power of words to connect, but of the three writers, he revealed less of himself to the world, choosing to let the words of poetry and scripture tell most of the story of God and humankind—and of himself in particular.

The symmetry of these writers' lives also shows a propensity for "staying put" finally in a community that wants to wrap its loving arms around each one of them as if safeguarding them from the homelessness of their youth, the darknesses of their pasts. Lou stayed in Charlotte where people could get to him when they needed him or he needed them, moving with Elizabeth to Southminster Retirement Community here in Charlotte. He continued his poetry readings in a lovely private dining room where his group of 10 or more gathered as if they were back in his study. He died in 2006 after living in Charlotte for 43 years; Tony stayed in Davidson, surrounded by a community who knew him, who could find him when they needed him or he needed them. Even after retiring from his tenure at Davidson College, he used his Davidson College office, and he had completed his new book of poems and sent it off to the publisher just before his death on October 3, 2020. Fred spends much time, even at age 94, in his home on the side of the Vermont mountain where he has lived for many years. He is known and loved in the community and can be found by friends and strangers alike (One of my favorite stories is one Goldie Stribling tells. She and husband Bruce were vacationing in Vermont, and, because she and the Buechners were friends, she planned to stop in and say hello. When they got to Rupert, that town of around 1500 people near the Buechners' home, Goldie and Bruce stopped to ask directions at the Post Office. When they asked a person there if she knew where Frederick Buechner lived, she said, "You mean Freddy?"). But we mustn't be fooled that these writers who found stability and room to be themselves in these fixed places were not keenly aware that for them there is another 'fixed' place beyond a church building, a college campus, a home on a mountainside. All their adult lives—and maybe in their childhoods, too—they had a homesickness for another home— the one God calls them to, the one where Jesus resides. To come through the joys and the darknesses that this life has to offer and still believe we are heading to that place of ultimate love—the one *everything* rushes toward in the Jessica Powers poem Lou liked—and that we get hints and glimpses of that world even while we live in this one, this is the strength of their gift to the world.

In much the same vein as Tony Abbott's story of that rifle shot which dissolved his family, Frederick Buechner's story of a dissolving family begins with the opening of a door. On an early Saturday morning in 1936, Fred, who was ten years old, and his brother Jamie, who was eight, were playing a game on the bed of their room when their father opened the door to look in on them. Then he closed it without speaking. The boys thought nothing of it at the time. They didn't even look up. When that door opened again, it was by the brothers who heard the shouts and cries of family members. The brothers discovered that their father Carl Frederick Buechner had ended his life in their closed garage filled with poisonous fumes. Fred says this about those moments in his memoir *The Sacred Journey* published in 1982:

"How long it was from the moment he closed that door to the moment we opened it, I no longer have any way of knowing, but the interlude can stand in a way for my whole childhood up till then and for everybody else's too, I suppose . . . From that moment to this I have ridden on time's back as a man rides a horse, knowing fully that the day will come when my ride will end and my time will end and all that I am and all that I have will end with them."(31)

Their lives would never be the same, and when Fred Buechner began his life as an author, that life begun in the tragedy of losing his earthly father weaved itself into the words he would choose. He says in his book *Eyes of the Heart*, "I suppose one way to read my whole life—my religious faith, the books I have written, the friends I have made—is as a search for him."(32)

Born on July 11, 1926, Frederick Buechner was born into a family with the German name Buechner, pronounced "Beekner" in the United States. His grandfather August Buechner had a silk-importing business that went under in 1929. Thereafter, they had to live on his wife's large inheritance. She, according to Fred, was a force to be reckoned with, "an unholy terror" throwing German words around like bolts of lightning, only to get over her anger as quickly as it had come. His mother, Katherine Kuhn, came from a fairly wealthy family, living in an elite gated community in East Liberty, PA, called Woodland Heights. When Fred, Sr. and Katherine eloped in 1922, Katherine's father did not speak to her for several years, but finally relented. Until that tragic day when Fred was ten, his father Fred, Sr. and Katherine moved from home to home and job to job, his father hoping to "find" his place in the world during those recession years. The marriage was not a stable one. In his memoir *The Sacred Journey*, the reader is told of episodes with his father when Fred noticed "something had gone terribly wrong with his laughter," and another time when his father wanted the keys to the car and his mother gave them to Fred, telling him his father "had had too much to drink and not to let him know where they were, no matter what."(33) That broken laughter led to the broken path his parents were on, the one that led to Fred, Sr.'s death and led his mother to the note found on the last page of *Gone with the Wind* that said, " I adore and love you," it said, "and am no good . . . Give Freddy my watch. Give Jamie my pearl pin. I give you all my love."(34)   Like Lou Patrick's uprootedness as an eleven-year-old, like Tony Abbott's loss of home at nine years old, Fred's world, already off-balance, changed even more with his mother's decision after her husband's death to move to Bermuda. Years later, when Fred Buechner's writing life was well under way, he described the year in Bermuda in his memoir. Thanks to the marvels of the internet, I found a 1936 video of life in Bermuda at that time. It matches Fred's descriptions of that place and its way of life at the time Fred entered its lush island surroundings and its English influence—horse drawn carriages called Victorias, bikes with their baskets evident everywhere you looked, a narrow-gauge railway as Fred called it,   English bobbies in uniforms and white helmets, and a place that invited sensual pleasures like the sounds of the rain, the smells of oleander and hibiscus blooms, and the sights of pastel houses with white roofs. Fred Buechner observed and remembered the year vividly. He was observant, yes, but when it came to his grief, he felt little of it.

" . . . the loss came to get buried so deep in me that after a time I scarcely ever took it out to look at it at all, let alone to speak of it. If ever anybody asked me how my father died, I would say heart trouble. That seemed at least a version of the truth. He had had a heart. It had been troubled. . . And then by grace or by luck or by some cool, child's skill for withdrawing from anything too sharp or puzzling to deal with, I stopped remembering so almost completely to remember at all that when, a year or so later, I came upon my brother crying one day all by himself in his room, I was stopped dead in my tracks. Why was he crying? When I prodded him into telling me that he was crying about something that he would not name but said only had happened a long time ago, I finally knew what he meant, and I can recapture still my astonishment that, for him, a wound was still open that for me, or so I thought, had long since closed. And in addition to the astonishment, there was also a shadow of guilt."(36)

We the readers are astonished by these words no less than the boy Fred Buechner was astonished by the revelation of his brother's feelings. How so like Tony Abbott's taking his "tears and putting them in his pocket with his used handkerchief." How like Lou Patrick's inability to speak much at all of his deepest grief, the loss of his son. Fred Buechner said in *Telling Secrets*, "Don't talk, don't trust, don't feel is supposed to be the unwritten law of families that for one reason or another have gone out of whack."(36) It is Fred's ability to use everyday language while talking about the hardest parts of life that share space with the most holy that resonates with readers. "Out of whack" hits our humanness. The words strike us as real. All humans deal with the shadow side of life, the darknesses that come to us all. No one escapes. But the wonder of it is that these three writers are willing as writers to look at the darkness, to recognize it in the writing of others, to write about it themselves, telling us all the while what they found in that profound darkness that lifted them up and could or would vicariously lift us as well. And what did they find? They found glimpses along the way of the love they sought, and they eventually found the calling of a loving God who was with them in the deep so that they, like the poet of Psalm 42, would not be afraid. Years later, when Fred read Shakespeare's *The Tempest*, he wrote that Caliban's speech about the island had haunted him all his life because it mirrors his remembrances of Bermuda. The lines start with "Be not affeard, the Isle is full of noyses,/ Sounds, and sweet aires, that give delight and hurt not." One cannot help comparing this line of comfort to the more than 350 times the Scriptures say, "Fear not." Signs like this, looked back on, of course, have directed Fred Buechner's journey. He believes this.

After the beginning of World War II, the three Buechners leave Bermuda, coming back to the mainland of the United States to reside in Tryon, NC, with Naya and Grandpa Kuhn who had retired there from Pittsburgh. It was Naya (called by that name for reasons even Fred Buechner has forgotten) who shaped him most profoundly in these early years. Here, just like in Bermuda, Fred stored up the things he would live out of in his adult life. Books and quirky neighbors and beauty and the sounds of Naya's voice telling him stories. The NC town of around 1500 people sits in the NC escarpment of the Blue Ridge Mountains, and when one walks the streets of that quaint town, one can feel even now what young Fred Buechner saw and heard then. The train tracks run right through the middle of the town, so he must have heard those lonesome whistles, the chugging engines, and the comings and goings of tourists and residents. The spring dogwoods and azaleas in colors pastel marked his way as he walked the streets. The building that housed Missildine's, a store he lovingly recalls in his memoirs, is still there. It was his beloved Naya, the person most attuned to his heartbeat, who took him and Jamie to the Episcopal Church and witnessed his christening even though no one in the family was particularly devout. Listen to how he puts it in *The Sacred Journey*:

" . . . to begin seeing anyway that there is pain in every life, even the apparently luckiest, that buried griefs and hurtful memories are part of us all . . . there is so much to see always, things too big to take in all at once, things so small as hardly to be noticed. And though they may well come by accident, these moments of our seeing, I choose to believe that it is by no means by accident when they open our hearts as well as our eyes . . . Who can ever foresee the crazy how and when and where of a grace that wells up out of the lostness and pain of the world and our own inner worlds?"(37)

What is apparent is that for Fred—and also for Lou and Tony—there was a deep-down-ness of their condition that would allow the holy to "well up" from those depths. Faith to these writers is similar in that this faith is a faith *in* something, even the unseen. This is the 'through-bearing' Lou Patrick mentioned in his 1956 sermon. But as children, says Fred in a lecture about Faith and Fiction, we often have to just live in this in-between time of figuring out our faith.

While the Buechners lived in Tryon, it was decided that Fred should go to the boarding school at the Lawrenceville School in New Jersey. Fred was enrolled in the school and his life *in* time began in earnest (as opposed to what Fred called the life 'below a time' of his childhood before the death of his father and the fairytale existence in Bermuda.). The Lawrenceville School in New Jersey became for Fred a place of stability much like Tony Abbott's Fay School in Massachusetts.

The details and timelines of a life as well documented as Fred Buechner's is easy to find. In Dale Brown's definitive look at the writings of Fred Buechner in *The Book of Buechner*, the same Dale Brown that founded The Buechner Institute, I often turn to the opening pages to find dates and events and book titles. I, like so many others, have read so many of Fred's writings that it helps to have a timeline of his works. I glance at it now: 1943—graduates from Lawrenceville; 1943-1944—Princeton University; 1944-1946—military service; 1946 1948—more Princeton years and graduation; 1948-1953—teacher of English at Lawrenceville School; 1950—publication of his first novel *A Long Day's Dying*.(38)

The *Newsweek* book reviewer of this first novel *A Long Day's Dying* mentions the fact that Fred Buechner has become "something of a literary sensation" because of "the mellow detachment of his point of view," along with the prose quality, the view of youth, and the book's organization. That detached point of view of the narrator would seem to echo Fred's adherence to close observation without emotional connection in his own life. One of the characters, the fat man Tristam Bone, shows up in later works in various iterations, making it easy for readers of his work to see some common themes while enjoying the vibrant characters. A subsequent novel, *The Seasons' Difference*, did not elicit the 'sensation' of the first one, however, and then, after a teaching stint at Lawrenceville, Fred moved to New York City to concentrate on his next novel. There, something happened. Something unexpected.

Fred used Sunday mornings to step out of his writing life and into the streets of New York. And sometimes he stopped into Madison Avenue Presbyterian Church, not so much because he liked going to church but rather because he had "nothing all that much better to do with my lonely Sundays."(39) He liked the sermons of the Rev. Dr. George Buttrick, the pastor there, particularly the fact that the listener could not easily guess what that preacher was going to come out with next. And then one Sunday, Buttrick preached a particular sermon that changed Fred's life. It came as a surprise, *the* surprise for Fred. Later in his life, Fred describes it this way in *The Sacred Journey*:

"Jesus Christ refused the crown that Satan offered him in the wilderness, Buttrick said, but he is king nevertheless because again and again he is crowned in the heart of the people who believe in him. And that inward coronation takes place, Buttrick said, 'among confession, and tears, and great laughter.' It was the phrase great laughter that did it, did whatever it was that I believe must have been hiddenly in the doing all the years of my journey up till then. It was not so much that a door

84

opened as that I suddenly found that a door had been open all along which I had only just then stumbled upon."(40)

As well-documented as Fred's journey is because he has chosen to share it in hopes that it speaks to the doors opening in all our journeys, I do not tire of reading his account. Why is that? It is precisely because it is particular and yet it resonates, making his particularity a signpost toward my own life journeys, moments in my own life "from beyond time" when, as Fred puts it, " something too precious to tell has glinted in the dusk, always just out of reach, like fireflies."(41)

The Jewish Rabbi Abraham Heschel said towards the end of his life, "What keeps me alive—spiritually, emotionally, intellectually—is my ability to be surprised." Fred was surprised; he was surprised again when years later he read a transcript from that sermon by George Buttrick and found that the phrase 'great laughter' was not there. From just such surprises hang the destinies of us all, Fred said. And it led him to the rest of his life to Union Theological Seminary, to becoming an ordained Presbyterian minister. He, like Lou, put all his yesterdays and tomorrows together and chose.

Fred Buechner's life as a writer of renown and as a person on a journey is as open and vulnerable as the open heart of Leo Bebb's church, Jesus's church, he writes about in his later novel *Open Heart*. This openness does not mean, however, that we see him completely any more than we see ourselves completely. There is always the mystery of what it means to be searching for "a self to be," as Fred puts it, a search "for other selves to love."(42) That kind of searching takes a lifetime—and possibly beyond. He says in an interview in a magazine entitled *Door,* 'It's sort of a continuing dim spectacle of the subterranean presence of grace in the world that haunts me. The mystery of mysteries at the bottom of the well, at the far reach of the road is the mystery of God, of Christ. This is what I explore." Fred Buechner, that journeyman who found others like Lou Patrick and Tony Abbott who willingly expressed their explorations of these fathomless mysteries, spares not himself in presenting these mysteries. After all, like Lou and Tony, he is quite aware of the deep-down-ness of things in that well, the darkness and shadow of that world along with lightnesses and joy. All three of these writers word for us what this journey takes and what it gives. In the last line in his 1970 book *Alphabet* of *Grace,* Fred prays, "Sweet Christ, forgive and mend. Of thy finally unspeakable grace, grant to each in his own dark room valor . . ."(43)

Back to the timeline of Fred Buechner's life, Dale Brown's book lists the years of seminary and ordination as a Presbyterian minister, his marriage to Judith Merck in 1956, his continuation of writing novels, his tenure as a teacher of religion at Philips Exeter Academy for about 10 years, the births of his three daughters Katherine, Dinah, and Sharman, and then the permanent move to Rupert, Vermont, in 1967 to pursue writing as a full-time endeavor. It is here that we take up the intertwined lives of Lou Patrick, Tony Abbott, and Fred Buechner. These three writers use words, write words, because it is who they are, and it is ultimately what many artists do when confronted by "the Ah of Wonder." If there is an inherent melancholy we feel when we read the stories of the darknesses confronted by these three men, if some readers dwell on the sadnesses these men faced, I picture the three of them saying, 'No, no, no!" It is not 'gloom and doom' when they explore the world both within and without, for out of these explorations comes laughter and joy and peace, which they gladly share with us.

It is at this time in Fred Buechner's writing life, the early 1970s, that he gave the lectures in Bangor, ME, and began the friendship with Lou Patrick and ultimately began the relationship with Trinity Presbyterian Church in Charlotte. Because of his relationship with Lou, Fred Buechner finally came to Montreat in 1980 (after much cajoling) as guest lecturer. Lou had been teaching Fred's books at Trinity for a while, so Fred and his writings were familiar to Lou's congregation. Part of what kept Fred from coming earlier was his fear of flying; he chose to lecture in places more easily reached by automobile. But come he finally did, and his lecture topic for the weekend is somewhat forgotten when placed beside the fact that he could not stay for the entire weekend, called away because his eldest daughter was gravely ill from anorexia, so ill that Fred had to 'fly' literally to her side. Sometime later, in November, he sent to Lou in printed form the sermon he would have given on Sunday morning in Montreat. At this most sorrowful time for Fred, this deep valley of darkness which finds him afraid, he sends a sermon and an accompanying letter to Trinity that echoes some of the themes that Lou Patrick used in his own sermon of 1956. The scripture for Fred's sermon is Lamentations 3:19-29 and John 16:16-25. The writer of Lamentations is in distress, his soul 'bowed down' in bitterness, and yet he praises the 'steadfast love of the Lord' whose mercies are 'new every morning.' The writer of Lamentations says of himself, "Let him sit alone in silence/ when he has laid [the yoke] on him;/ let him put his mouth in the dust —/ there may yet be hope;"

Fred must have been feeling like this writer, feeling like the psalmist who cries to God and longs for him in Psalm 42.

In the sermon that came with the letter, Fred quotes Dostoevsky's novel *The Brothers Karamazov*, in which the youngest brother Alyosha is present at the vigil for an old monk named Zossima who has died; Alyosha is hoping for a miracle from God that will send a sign that God is present. A sign might be that Zossima does not decay like others. But Alyosha gets only the stench of "decay and death," so he is ready to give up on hope of miracle as he keeps vigil. Then he falls asleep. He has a dream about the wedding in Cana. Fred quotes this part of the novel.

"It is the marriage, the wedding," Dostoevsky writes. "There are the guests, there are the young couple sitting, the wise governor of the feast, and suddenly there is old Zossima too— a little thin old man with tiny wrinkles on his face, his ancient glittering eyes, and of all the things he could be doing, what he is doing in that dream is laughing, laughing at that great feast like a child. And when Alyosha wakes up, he does something that he himself does not fully understand. He tears out of the chapel and rushes down into the monastery yard. He hears inside himself the words, 'Water the earth with the tears of your joy and love those tears' and suddenly he gets down on all fours and kisses the earth with his lips: and when he gets up, he's no longer a teary wreck of a boy but a 'champion.'

Fred then quotes Lamentations again. He goes on in the sermon: "You've got to watch out for these prophets and preachers, these novelists Russian and otherwise. They are apt to get so carried away by what they're saying that we are in danger of getting carried away with them—this marvelous picture of sober, clear-headed people like you and me leaving this church in a few minutes from now and making clowns of ourselves by getting down on all fours in our Sunday-go-to-meeting best, and kissing the mucked-up sod of Montreat, North Carolina."

Reynolds Price once said in a review, "It is Buechner's big strength that he is so lucidly particular." In this sermon, Fred's language is so particular that his listeners are addressed as if invited into a warm room; he, like Lou Patrick, searches for the exact word rather than a mere word. The John 16 passage used for this sermon reminds us of God's presence, just as Jesus reminded his disciples that "there is no depth of human need where we cannot see him both needing us and reaching out to our need" even though at best we see dimly in hints and glimpses. This passage is reminiscent of Lou's 1956 sermon in which he says, "It is human, but foolish, to cry out, Does God care? Look at Calvary if you want to see how much he cares. You see, what is happening there is happening to God . . . He is that much at one with us in the very depth of our needs."

This sermon of Fred's has echoes in Tony Abbott's poem "The Beloved Son" based on the parable in Mark 12. Tony imagines in the poem that the father of the parable mourns the death of his son killed by the tenants of his vineyard:

"He measured his hatred in hours. . .
But then the angel came, or something
like the angel, something in the night
in dreams . . . 'forgive . . . they know not
what they're doing . . .'
What will the owner of the vineyard do?
I see him kneeling at the dark gate
in the mud, soft after the spring rains.
'Pray with me,' he calls to the tenants.
'This is the body of my son, broken
for you.' And he reaches high, holding
in his hands the blue mantle, and the tenants
come forth, weeping, and the father takes
each of them in his arms and kisses them."(44)

Deep calls unto deep at the thunder of thy cataracts," says the Psalmist. Fred, along with Lou and Tony, knows the depths of sorrow carried by humans, but he also offers in his own words and in his own life the good news that we are not alone. God with us is the message. He mentions as well that this message takes the form of the reaching out of humans to humans. Listen to some of his letter to the Trinity congregation that accompanied that written sermon of 1980:

> *"I, Buechner, called by great laughter and the rattling of a tree to be a fool for Christ, to all of you in Charlotte who have been summoned also to wear our Saviour's motley, grace be unto you and peace from God our father and the Lord Jesus Christ. As many of you know, the time I was with you was a darkly troubled one for me and my family, a time of great foreboding and grief. In your promise to pray for me and mine, I found hope. And praise be to God all your prayers together with ours seem to have been heard because for the moment at least the crisis appears to have passed and things are better than they were. But the road ahead still lies deep in shadow, and I beg you to continue to remember us as we make our way along it . . . There can be no one of you who does not do hard and lonely battle against the dark times that menace us all in a world which so often God seems to have forgotten and which with such dark skill manages to hide God from us. So whatever your doubts, whatever your pain, whatever your fear, my prayer is that God of his mercy and grace will strengthen you with the knowledge that he grieves with you in all your grieving and that no matter how you resist him and seem to lose him and no matter how the world thwarts him, in the end his saving will be unimaginably and blessedly done.*

What an astounding letter. . . a beginning which references the beginnings of Paul's letters in the Bible, but more to the point references how well we at Trinity knew some of his writings. We had heard about his conversion experience. We had read his novels and his theological writings. We knew about the apple tree (more on this later). Fred's darkness is lifted somewhat with regard to his daughter's slow recovery, and Trinity rejoiced with him. Trinity kept and cherished this letter and the sermon, this personal affirmation of Fred's hopeful belief that even in the darkest of times, he was not alone.

In 1984, Lou invited Fred to come again and to read in Trinity's sanctuary in Charlotte, NC. Through his novels, his sermons, his prolific published works, Fred's words had reached a large following. Pastors from pulpits around the world were quoting him (often mispronouncing his name), people from all over were trying to entice him off his mountain in Vermont. Come down, they wrote. Come let us hear your voice, *the* voice behind these words. For the rather reserved Fred Buechner, these pleas must have been hard. But come he did to many who called. He came to Trinity because his friend asked him to. Rarely since the days Lou offered those Christmas Eve services has the Trinity Sanctuary been filled to overflowing. Trinity folk pulled out all the red carpets (or yellow brick roads) they could for Fred's arrival. A reservation-only dinner in the Fellowship Hall was transformed into the Land of Oz because of Fred's love of the books by L. Frank Baum. Bless his good heart, Fred endured it all for Lou's sake, for our sakes, maybe for God's sake. I think back upon it—I, dressed as

92

Dorothy, my husband Dale as Tin Man, my four-year-old son Daniel as Toto, others as Scarecrow and Cowardly Lion, and rainbows everywhere—and I wonder how he climbed those steps into the pulpit afterwards, having anything left to speak out over the people in the pews. On April 9, 1984, *The Charlotte Observer* reviewer Terry Mattingly wrote about Fred's appearance in Charlotte, calling him a "shy-looking minister with a sleepy voice." Goodness, this description of his voice makes me hope Fred did not ever read this review, mainly because the timbre of Fred Buechner's voice sounds so much like music that it, above almost all the voices I have ever heard, is the one I hear in my head when I am reading scripture or novels or essays. Lou Patrick said the same thing—that he heard Fred's voice as he himself read poetry. Ah, well, we are all trying to word what can't be easily worded, and often for Fred he is writing and speaking about the ineffable quality of God in the world. The reviewer did capture the high points of the message Fred brought that night: "People must keep the doors of their hearts open to the 'extraordinary within the ordinary.'" Fred also mentioned his now-famous line about paying attention to our lives, one of the first quotes to pop up on any website about Fred Buechner. The message Fred brings about paying attention is that there are angels amongst us, and we are unaware they are there to bring messages . . . words God wants us to hear about ourselves and the world around us. This is good news, even in the darkest of times. Like the young girl in the Dickens novel who says to Sidney Carlton, "I believe God sent you to me" that Lou used in his 1956 sermon. Like the spirit of Tony Abbott's daughter, the muse of his writing, who, along with the girl in the yellow raincoat, brings some healing. Fred's belief that God uses the ordinary to show us the extraordinary is manifested over and over in his writings. And his life.

During the writing of the novel *Godric,* the most beloved and acclaimed of Fred's books, Fred's own life was in that particularly dark place as his family helped his daughter battle anorexia. That real 12th century English monk's remarkable life, recorded in a Latin manuscript, is the tale of a man who lived a secular life for fifty years before giving his heart to God and living the next fifty years as an anchorite-type of hermit living next to the River Wear. The writing about that saint served as a saving grace for Fred as mysterious as any of God's tender mercies. There was even the arrival of a stranger who came to Vermont, a professor of a family member who came to visit, who helped him translate that Latin manuscript for Fred. It was during this time that Fred had had to leave Montreat the first time he was there. It was soon after, after Fred had discovered that not only could he not save his daughter himself but that his love for her might even have been standing in the way of her healing, that Fred, back home to Vermont, opened the door to find Lou Patrick on his doorstep, unannounced, uninvited; just there. Fred would have been praying, praying hard for his daughter's healing, but perhaps he, like Saint Godric, was asking himself this: "What's prayer? It's shooting shafts into the dark. What mark they strike, if any, who's to say? It's reaching for a hand you cannot touch."(45) Into the middle of Fred's darkness, came a hand to touch.

Really. He has written that that friend on his doorstep with no agenda and no words, with just a presence, was indeed sent from God. Afterward, in a June 8, 1981, letter to Lou, Fred says this about God:

> *". . . and part of the adventure, it just begins to dawn on me— and maybe even the most important part and the part with vast stores of light and blessing in it—has been the growing realization of how richly and profoundly I have been ministered to. That sounds so churchy and unreal to my hopelessly secular ears. The language of it; but the truth of it is unavoidable. . . God's jokes are so big and simple that nobody gets them . . . I am just beginning to get at least one of them, which is that, yes, when you are desperate, he comes to you as he always said he would, sends his servants to you, to serve you, to heal and help. He sent me most especially you—can I say that without causing you embarrassment?*

Later in the letter, he writes about his desire to run away.

> *I had a desperate impulse to go away somewhere for a while for everybody's sake . . . I came within an inch of phoning you and saying could you possibly go off on a trip with me somewhere— to Durham, England, or Disneyland—or could I come down to Charlotte for a while to clean up the Sunday school rooms or drive old ladies to church. . . but my job is here. . . maybe someday, when the clouds lift, there could be such a time. Do you suppose? Anyway—how lovely to be writing you, to have you to write to. With blessings always, Fred."*

"To lend to each other a hand when we're falling . . .Perhaps that's the only work that matters in the end."(46) Fred Buechner has Saint Brendan say this in his 1987 book *Brendan*, his novel about another saint, this time from 6th century Ireland. This 'hand' Lou lent Fred, a real hand that was attached to the real person of Lou Patrick on the real doorstep is mentioned again in correspondence between these friends— Fred asking Lou to visit in the summer of 1981 on the occasion of his 60th birthday, "when it might be especially comforting to have you on hand," and another time saying, "This letter has no point other than to reach out and clasp your hand." In a letter from January of 1981, Fred says about himself and Lou: "I see us arm in arm in striped blazers and straw boaters doing an off-to-Buffalo shuffle behind the footlights. Nor is that so far from the truth when you get right down to it. I only wish it could be arm in arm more often."

These words of strength are echoed in Fred's writings over and over. He says, in another letter in May of 1981. *"In the midst of all the darkness, I was more aware than I think I've ever been before of the presence and grace and mystery of God somewhere at the heart of it."* In a sermon on the stewardship of pain published in his compilation book *Secrets in the Dark*, he says, "We are never more in touch with life than when life is painful, never more in touch with hope than we are then, if only the hope of another human presence to be with us and for us."(47) The gift of Fred Buechner is that he words for us over and over again, even in the midst of his own pain, the comfort and faith in a God who is with us. Fred freely gives us himself, and therefore gives us an image of God. Or maybe it is the other way around—he gives us his God and therefore himself.

Are we not lifted up ourselves by the truth of these words? I picture these two giants of the written word, Fred and Lou, clasping hands the way I clasp the hands of the friends and sometimes strangers who are extraordinarily present in my life and have been so in some of the darkest times. It is God's doing, I choose to believe, sending these answers to prayer, answers to something deep within us.

&

So. What can I say finally about these things, about these writers who are intertwined in myriad ways? First, I think, is how Lou Patrick, Tony Abbott, and Fred Buechner love God's world and all that was created therein. They give God the power and glory and goodness, and secondly, they pray that God grants them the valor to journey towards him, to recognize him in the through-bearing. And finally, they realize that they, like everyone else, are always falling but always heading for home, to that other home they have had only glimpses of here.

In his 1965 novel *The Final Beast,* Fred's main character Nick is lying down under apple trees, waiting for a sign that God exists, that Jesus will come.

"Please," he whispered. Still flat on his back, he stretched out his fists as far as they would reach—"Please . . ."—then opened them, palms up, and held them there as he watched for something, for the air to cleave, fold back like a tent flap, to let a splendor through. You prayed to the Christ in the people you knew, the living and the dead: what should you do, who should you be? And sometimes they told you. But to pray now this other prayer, not knowing what you were asking, only "Please, please . . ." Somewhere a screen door slammed, and all the leaves were still except for one that fluttered like a bird's wing.

"Please come," he said, then "Jesus," swallowing, half blind with the sun in his eyes as he raised his head to look. The air would part like a curtain, and the splendor would not break or bend anything but only fill the empty places between the trees, the trees and the house, between his hands which he brought together now. "Fear not," he thought. He was not afraid. Nothing was happening… He listened for "Feed my sheep… feed my lambs…"

Two apple branches struck against each other with the limber clack of wood on wood. That was all—a tick-tock rattle of branches—but then a fierce lurch of excitement at what was only daybreak, only the smell of summer coming, only starting back again for home, but oh Jesus, he thought with a great lump in his throat and a crazy grin, it was an agony of gladness and beauty falling wild and soft like rain. Just clack-clack, but praise him, he thought. Praise him. Maybe all his journeying, he thought, had been only to bring him here to hear two branches hit each other twice like that, to see nothing cross the threshold but to see the threshold, to hear the dry clack-clack of the world's tongue at the approach of the approach perhaps of splendor.

He sat up, clasping his knees in his arms. Someone was calling, "Nick oh Nick . . . and as he watched, wooden-throated, a neat, dark figure appeared around the corner of his father's house. "Denbigh!" It came out an unfamiliar croak and he tried again. "As I live and breathe." Denbigh did not see him at first . . . then he came trotting through the high weeds. "Nick, old man! Your dad said he saw you out here through the window, and there you are." There was the handsome little flash of a smile as he shook his hand. . ."(48)

To see the extraordinary in the ordinary. To give or receive a hand. To use Godric's words, "Praise God for all that's holy, cold, and dark."(49) This is a sign of something of Heaven right here, the not-alone-ness in the middle of the valley of the shadow of death. And when this world of humans seems to fail, there is the healing world of God's creation that speaks to us in its "clack-clack" of apple branches, and, when we are blind to that, the gift is that God promises to be with us in the shadows of our deepest longings, the thunder of his voice sounding like silence sometimes.

"Comfort me with apples" says the poet of Song of Solomon in the Bible. Fred's belief in his character Nick being given a sign through the apple tree branches was with him always, was with him as he addressed the Trinity congregation in that letter of 1980, was with him as he wrote words straight into the hearts of his readers, so much so that one Trinity member gave him NC apple branches during a visit in Charlotte to carry back to Vermont.

Tony Abbott wrote about this same comfort in a poem called "Remembrance" written in 1993, a poem that addresses great loss. It begins and ends with spring:

"The spring rises from the earth, root to stem
blossom to leaf. Each day catches the breath
like a song remembered, forgotten then found
again. . .

You rise like the season. Your face shines
in the pools along the road as I walk
to the grave yard. I pass the old house.
You glide down the stairs and take my hand.
We share the season. Is it hyacinth or lilac
I smell? I lie in the grass beside your stone.
I watch the bees work in the crossed branches
of the blooming apple tree. The sky shines beyond.

I bring you my anger and my pain. I hand
them to you like bread. I speak the loaves
of my sorrow, the broken pieces of my rage . . .

Now I hug the earth, pressing my chest to the
growing grass, spreading my arms outward. I close
my eyes and wait. The anger drains like water after rain. . . "Sit,"
you say,
and I squat with you cross-legged like some
novice guru. "Kneel," you say, and the stone
cuts the letters of your name into the memory

of my knees. "Eat," you say, and my mouth opens like the
yawning bird's. "Taste," you say,
and your love charms the buds of my tongue.

I rise like one groggy after dreaming. I stagger
homeward on the cracked sidewalk into the back yard of the
old house. Everywhere, in the knee-high
grass, spring flowers bloom madly."(50)

Tony's comfort from the hyacinth and lilacs and crossed apple
blossom branches which bring a presentiment of new life will
have to be enough for us, just like the clack-clack of apple
branches in the story Fred describes in his novel *The Final Beast*.
There is comfort, now, all around us in this life, if we but see
that the extraordinary *is* the ordinary. As Fred has Godric say
to humankind about how he has filled the last fifty years of his
life: "Three things I've filled it with: *what used to be, what might
have been, and for the third, what may be yet* and in some measure *is*
already had we only eyes to see."(51) "Deep calls unto deep at
the thunder of thy cataracts." If this be true, if the calling of
God is to be with us, then he is in that pocket of tears with the
used handkerchief when Tony was a child—and evermore. He
is with Fred when he opens that door as a ten-year-old—and
evermore. And he is with Lou as he loses a home and later
when he loses a son—and evermore. Lou once preached a
Thanksgiving message with the title "Comfort Me With
Apples." He uses that phrase from Song of Solomon, that
voice of the female poet being wooed by the one she loves:

"As an apple tree among the trees of the wood,
so is my beloved among young men.
With great delight I sat in his shadow,
and his fruit was sweet to my taste.
He brought me to the banqueting house,
and his banner over me was love.
Sustain me with raisins,
comfort me with apples."

Lou uses this scripture to preach on Thanksgiving and the things to be grateful for. But he points out that although we seem to be always "looking for the good life, we need to start with the faith that life *is* good." Lou writes that scriptures "sing to us another song, a 'comfort me with apples' song. It sings of simple things. It gives us a poem not about "things" that we acquire ourselves but rather gifts of ordinariness like apples. ". . . let me be the kind of person who can be comforted with apples. Let my life be so full that the addition of one simple thing can cause it to overflow with joy." Lou wrote about the fullness of life here and now that comes when one acknowledges the profound gifts of God and his promise to us that he will be with us even now—and evermore.

Now. And ever shall be. Each of these writers—Lou, Tony, and Fred—have chosen words that give us a hint as to the person he is or the one he searches to be. And one thing more: they give us a glimpse of a home we are all moving toward. One that deep down we are homesick for.

In that 1996 dialogue with Lou, I naively wanted Dorothy in *The Wizard of Oz* to get home again because "there's no place like home" as she says at the end of Judy Garland's 1939 movie, and I, with so many others I suspect, want the same feeling. But Lou answers me:

"We all have a longing to get home but we're talking about a home that is not available in terms of being a child again . . . It's not available in terms of being in the same place any more than we can be in the same time anymore. It's something for which we have hints and glimpses only. But we know we are homesick. Deep down, any night we sit out and look at the stars, we either get this feeling we are in an alien universe or of being on our way to something we have never yet seen or heard, to something that has not yet entered into our understanding."

I think Lou chooses, and puts all his hopes and dreams, his yesterdays and tomorrows, in this idea that we are on the way to God. That's why he liked that poem about everything rushing to God.

Tony Abbott reminds us of this idea in his poem "To Have Been There" in his book of poetry *The Dark Side of North*:

TO HAVE BEEN THERE

For this is the will of my Father, that everyone who sees the Son and believes in him should have eternal life; and I will raise him up at the last day. John 6:40

I have been thinking about eternal life,
about what happens when we die,
about what belief means. Somehow
before, it was less important.
I always used to say eternal life was

God's problem, not ours. It was all
a matter of grace. If you believed,
it was a gift. You couldn't control it.
You couldn't worry about it, you
couldn't make it happen.

Faith is God's business, that's what
I always used to say. Our business is to love.
But now it's bigger than that, more than that.
I can't grasp it. Here is Jesus, in Capernaum,
he's taken the boat from Tiberias, slipped
away, and the people, desperate to find him,
have climbed into their fishing boats and rowed,
sailed, I don't know, to Capernaum. And he
tells them that if they believe, they will have
eternal life. And the Pharisees murmured

against him, isn't that wonderful? Murmured.
And Jesus says, "Do not murmur among
yourselves." I love that. I can see the scene.
The Pharisees saying, this is Joseph,
the carpenter's son. How can he give eternal

life to anyone? But there it is, there it is.
Eternal life, for the grasping, the hand
reaching toward Jesus, touching him. I believe,
you say, I believe, because I want it so badly.

Wanting to live forever, here, there, wherever
there is life. To have it never stop. There is Jesus,
standing on the corner in his hometown,

the Pharisees murmuring, and the people,
that's the point, the people, staring,
mouths open, tears in their eyes. They have been
changed by this man who opens his mouth
and everything is different. Everything.

That's what eternal life is, that everything—
isn't it, that everything transformed
into light, into joy, into the love that needs
nothing more."(52)
Transformation. Resurrection. Remembrance. Homesickness.
Heaven. Words. Jesus. God.

Not just words, but a desire to write and say and hear *the* word.
Fred puts it like this in his memoir *Now and Then*:

> " ... to listen... for the sound, above all else, of his
> voice. Because the word that God speaks to us is
> always an incarnate word . . . We are so used to hearing
> what we want to hear and remaining deaf to what it
> would be well for us to hear that it is hard to break the

habit. But if we keep our hearts and minds open as well as our ears, if we listen with patience and hope, if we remember at all deeply and honestly, then I think we come to recognize, beyond all doubt, that, however faintly we may hear him, he is indeed speaking to us, and that, however little we may understand of it, his word to each of us is both recoverable and precious beyond telling."(53)

In *The Eyes of the Heart*, Fred Buechner's elderly mother asked him whether he believed anything happened after death. I think Fred's mother asked out of the deep-down-ness of what it means to be human and in her case facing one's end in this world. She asked it for me, as well. And Fred's answer was one he wrote down in a letter to his mother later that day. His letter was to me, as well. For you, too.

"I wrote her I believe that what happens when you die is that, in ways I knew no more about than she did, you are given back your life again, and I said there were three reasons why I believed it. First, I wrote her, I believed it because, if I were God and loved the people I created and wanted them to become at last the best they had it in them to be, I couldn't imagine consigning them to oblivion when their time came with the job under the best of circumstances only a fraction done. Second, I said, I believed it, apart from any religious considerations, because I had a hunch it was true. I intuited it . . . It feels as though, at the innermost heart of it, there is Holiness . . . we belong to Holiness. . . And lastly, I wrote her, I believe that what happens to us after we die is that we aren't dead forever because Jesus said so . . . In one way Jesus was a human being like the rest of us . . . But when he said to the Good Thief on the cross next to him, "Today shalt thou be with me in Paradise," I wrote her, I would bet my bottom dollar that he of all people knew what he was talking about, because if in one way he was a human being, in another way he was immeasurably more."(54)

The comfort of the words from these three writers whose lives are intertwined quicken *my* life. These three men bet all their yesterdays and tomorrows on not just words, but *the* word. They give me hope in things unseen— when I am afraid or in darkness, or when I am glad because of the simplest of joys in this life—the hope can't be overstated. Truly. I have memorized many of their words so that I may use them in conversations with others who are willing to discuss such things. I use them because I am trying to believe them. I am trying to have valor for the through-bearing and tears, and also for the joys of a delicious apple or a haunting piece of music or my children's lives or the love I feel for or receive from another person. I use them because I want to praise the source of these words that well up from deep within. I want to praise God because, even faintly, even if it was just once upon a time, I heard him calling to me.

Deep calls unto deep at the thunder of thy cataracts.

Janet Vass Sarjeant

Notes

1. Brueggemann, Walter. *Praying the Psalms*. Winona: Saint Mary's Press, 1986, p. 17.
2. Buechner, Frederick. *The Sacred Journey*. San Francisco: Harper & Row, 1982.
3. Dillard, Annie. *Pilgrim at Tinker Creek*. New York: Harper Perennial, 1998, p. 274.
4. Willimon, William, Ed. *Sermons From the Duke Chapel*. Durham: Duke University Press, 2005, p. 238.
5. Ibid., p. 237.
6. Ibid., p. 240.
7. Buechner, Frederick. *Telling Secrets*. New York: HarperSanFrancisco, 1991. p 2-3.
8. Powers, Jessica. "Everything Rushes." *Selected Poetry of Jessica Powers*. Regina Siegfried and Robert Morneau, eds. Kansas City, MO: Sheed & Ward, 1989.
9. Berry, Wendell. "Boone." *New Collected Poems*. Berkley: Counter Point, 2012.
10. Abbott, Anthony. "In Grand Central Station." *If Words Could Save Us*. Davidson: Lorimer Press, 2011.
11. Abbott, Anthony. *Leaving Maggie Hope*. Charlotte: Novello Festival Press, 2003, p.177.
12. Abbott, Anthony. "The Boy From Somewhere Else." *Dark Side of North*. Press 53: Winston-Salem. 2020, p.11.
13. Buechner, Frederick. *Longing For Home*. New York: HarperCollins, 1996, p. 23.
14. Abbott, Anthony. *Leaving Maggie Hope*. Charlotte: Novello Festival Press, 2003, p. 25.
15. Abbott, Anthony. *The Angel Dialogues*. Davidson: Lorimer Press, 2014.
16. Abbott, Anthony. *The Three Great Secret Things*. Charlotte: Main Street Rag Publishing Company, 2007, pp. 3-4.

17.   Abbott, Anthony. "The Girl in The Yellow Raincoat." *The Girl in the Yellow Raincoat.* Laurinburg: St. Andrews Press, 1989, p. 1.

18.   Abbott, Anthony. "Up the Rabbit Hole or Oz Revisited." *The Girl in the Yellow Raincoat.* Laurinburg: St. Andrews Press, 1989, p. 52.

19.   Eliot, T.S. "Little Gidding." *T.S. Eliot Collected Poems.* New York: Harcourt Brace Jovanovich, 1991, p. 208.

20.   Buechner, Frederick. *Telling the Truth.* San Francisco: Harper & Row, 1977, p.96-97.

21.   Buechner, Frederick. *Open Heart.* New York: Atheneum, 1972, pp. 100-101.

22.   Buechner, Frederick. *Magnificent Defeat.* New York: The Seabury Press, 1979, p. 26.

23.   Abbott, Anthony S. "Before Forty." *The Girl in the Yellow Raincoat.* Laurinburg: St. Andrews Press, 1989, p. 62.

24.   Abbott, Anthony S. "Jamie's Prayer." *Dark Side of North.* Winston-Salem: Press 53, 2020, p. 47.

25.   Abbott, Anthony S. "The Angel Thinks of Music." *The Angel Dialogues.* Davidson: Lorimer Press, 2014, p. 57.

26.   Abbott, Anthony S. "The Angel Speaks of Death." *The Angel Dialogues.* Davidson: Lorimer Press, 2014, p. 60.

27.   Abbott, Anthony S. "Dark Side of North." *Dark Side of North.* Winston-Salem: Press 53, 2020, p. xxi.

28.   Abbott, Anthony S. "A Poem For My Daughter on Her Fiftieth Birthday." Dark Side of North. Winston-Salem: Press 53, 2020, p.3.

29.   Eliot, T.S. "Dry Salvages." *T.S. Eliot Collected Poems.* New York: Harcourt Brace Jovanovich, 1991, p. 197.

30.   Buechner, Frederick. *Sacred Journey.* San Francisco: Harper & Row, 1982, p. 6.

31.   Ibid, p. 39.

32. Buechner, Frederick. *The Eyes of the Heart.* New York: HarperCollins, 1999, p. 23-24.
33. Buechner, Frederick. *Sacred Journey.* San Francisco: Harper & Row, 1982, p. 33.
34. Ibid., p. 41.
35. Ibid., p. 41-42.
36. Buechner, Frederick. *Telling Secrets.* San Francisco: HarperSanFrancisco, 1991, p. 10.
37. Buechner, Frederick. *Sacred Journey.* San Francisco: Harper & Row, 1982, p. 56-57.
38. Brown, Dale. *The Book of Buechner.* Louisville: Westminster John Knox Press, 2006, p. xiii-xviii.
39. Buechner, Frederick. *Sacred Journey.* San Francisco: Harper & Row, 1982, p. 108.
40. Ibid., p. 109.
41. Ibid., p. 111.
42. Ibid., p. 72.
43. Buechner, Frederick. Alphabet of Grace. London: Walker and Company, 1970, p. 141.
44. Abbott, Anthony. "The Beloved Son." If Words Could Save Us. Davidson: Lorimer Press, 2011, p. 64.
45. Buechner, Frederick. *Godric.* New York: Atheneum, 1980, p. 142.
46. Buechner, Frederick. *Brendan.* New York: Atheneum, 1987, p. 217.
47. Buechner, Frederick. *Secrets in the Dark.* San Francisco: HarperSanFrancisco, 2006, p. 216.
48. Buechner, Frederick. *The Final Beast.* New York: Atheneum, 1965, p. 176-177.
49. Buechner, Frederick. *Godric.* New York: Atheneum, 1980, p. 96.
50. Abbott, Anthony S. "Remembrance." *A Small Thing Like a Prayer.* Laurinburg: St. Andrews Press, 1993, p. 73.

51. Buechner, Frederick. *Godric.* New York: Atheneum, 1980, p. 139.
52. Abbott, Anthony S. "To Have Been There." *Dark Side of North.* Davidson: Lorimer Press, 2020, p. 34.
53. Buechner. Frederick. *Now and Then.* San Francisco: HarperSanFrancisco, 1983, p. 3.
54. Buechner, Frederick. *The Eyes of the Heart.* San Francisco: HarperSanFrancisco, 1999, pp. 14-16.

CPSIA information can be obtained
at www.ICGtesting.com
Printed in the USA
JSHW042342260621
16315JS00002B/11